A Voice From The Lost Town Of Trochenbrod

Cherry Orchard Books

A Voice From the Lost Town of Trochenbrod

A TRANSLATION OF YISRAEL BEIDER'S POEMS, ESSAYS, AND LETTERS

Translated from the Hebrew by
Gabriel Laufer

Some translation from Yiddish by
Andrew Cassel and Ellen Cassedy

2025

Library of Congress Control Number: 2024047604

Copyright © Academic Studies Press, 2025

ISBN 9798887196619 hardback
ISBN 9798887196626 paperback
ISBN 9798887196633 ebook PDF
ISBN 9798887196640 epub

Book design by PHi Business Solutions
Cover design by Andrea Liss

Published by Cherry Orchard Books, an imprint of
Academic Studies Press
1007 Chestnut Street
Newton, MA 02464
press@academicstudiespress.com
www.academicstudiespress.com

Contents

Yisrael Beider and His Literary Work	xi
Trochenbrod, the Town That Was	xix
Acknowledgements	xxxvii
Notes on the Text	xxxix

1. POEMS   1

Nature   3

A Winter Poem	3
From the Valley	4
Cloudlets	6
Winter in the Countryside	9
On the Farm	11
Frost	12
Between Trickles	13
A Note from the Countryside	14
Alone	16
Alien [country]	17
On the Way to the Village	19
In the Village	24
The Old Doc	35
Beneath the Crescent Moon	37
Spring Has Run Away...	39

The Land of Israel   43

On the Edge	43
Who Is the Hebrew!	44

Excursion in the Homeland   45
Lamentations   48
"Der Pastukh"—The Shepherd   51

Family   53
Father's Home   53
Work   59
Sarah is Departing   63
Motherly Bliss   65
The Photograph   66
To Ya'akov   67
You are Bar Mitzvah . . .   70

Oppression   73
When the Eighth Candle Dies Out   73
The Orphan   74
From the Abyss   77
On the Water   80
In a Foreign Land   81
At the Ice Rink   83
The Fair   84

Old Age   85
Old Age   85
At My Setting Sun   91

Miscellaneous   92
Untitled   92
The Jealousy Is Eating Me   93
Untitled   95

If for Each Failure of Mine	96
Ashmedai	97

2. ESSAYS — 99

Jerusalem	101
The Modest One	107
Today Is Tisha'a be-Av	110
The Abbreviator, of Blessed Memory (A Khasidic Story)	115
Rambam and His Gentile Adversary (A Folk Legend)	124
A Drop in the Sea (From the Recent Past)	129
Without Bialik	144
A Jewish Heart... Memories from the Recent Past	147

3. LETTERS — 155

Letter to His Brother Hayim	157
Letter to Hayim	160
Letter to His Brother Hayim or Hagai	169
Letter to Hayim	176
Letter to an Unnamed Friend in Międzyrzecz	180
Letter to His Brother Shimon	184
Letter to His Brothers Zalman and Naftali [on the Death of Shimon]	188
Eulogy	195
Letter to His Mother	198

References	203
Appendix: Yisrael Beider's Family Tree, June 28, 2012	204

When I am dead eulogize me so:
"There was a man—and look: he is no more;
Before his time this man died,
The song of his life ceased midway;
Too bad! He still had one song—
And now that song is eternally lost,
Eternally lost!"

From "When I am Dead," by Hayim Nahman Bialik, 1904

Yisrael Beider and His Literary Work

By Gabriel Laufer, Avrom Bendavid-Val, and Ilene Vogelstein

Nearly eighty years after the Holocaust swept away the Ukrainian Jews, we continue to discover forgotten tragic stories and lost literary works of unique quality and creativity. Two of those are the story of the lost town of Trochenbrod, an exclusively Jewish town, and the life work of one of its sons, Yisrael Beider. The two were lost late in the summer and fall of 1942. The town of Trochenbrod was totally eradicated, erased without a trace, and its citizens murdered. Yisrael Beider and his two sons were murdered either in Trochenbrod, Olyka,[1] or Międzyrzecz (pronounced Mezeritch);[2] we may never know.

Trochenbrod was and still is revealing its past stories to a handful of survivors and their descendants.[3] But most victims in this all-Jewish town died without leaving a trace; taken to

---

1 A small town near Trochenbrod, east of Lutsk, Ukraine.
2 A city in western Poland approximately five hundred miles from Trochenbrod.
3 Avrom Bendavid-Val, *The Heavens Are Empty: Discovering the Lost Town of Trochenbrod* (New York: Pegasus Books, 2011).

a remote forest, ordered undressed, lined up along a pit and shot dead, taking with them their names, likeness, life stories, thoughts, ideas, and creativity. The destruction was so complete that even if a photo surfaced, there may not be anyone left alive to identify its subjects. Mass graves scattered all over Ukraine are all that is left of approximately 1.5 million Jews that once lived, loved, hoped, created.

Though we might never know the time and place of his death, and certainly not his last resting place, Yisrael Beider left behind a unique collection of poems, essays, and letters that describe the life he experienced in rural Ukraine and in Trochenbrod[4] in the years between the two world wars. It sheds light on the life of Jews subjected to *pogroms*, abuse, and abject poverty. But at the same time, his work brings to life lovingly beautiful images of nature, rich Jewish culture, and yearnings for the Land of Israel. This is a rare first-hand account of life in Trochenbrod and its neighboring towns as the sun was about to set on the Jewish existence there.

Yisrael Beider was born in 1895 in Verba, Ukraine, to Rabbi Moshe David Pearlmutter.[5] As a descendant of thirteen

---

4   Though at that time Trochenbrod and its surroundings were part of a greater Poland that location is now in western Ukraine.
5   Rabbi Pearlmutter was born as Moshe David Plesser and changed his name before his fourth child (Shimon) was born so that the male baby could be registered as first born, thus avoiding conscription to the Russian army. The law was enacted by the Tsar Nicholas I as means to assimilate the Jews (Vainer Ya'akov et al., eds., *Ha-Ilan ve-Shorashav: Sefer Korot Tal: Zofyovka—Ignatovka* [Giv'atayim: Agudat Bet Tal, 1988]). Pearlmutter later changed his name again to Beider. Consequently, some of Beider's siblings go by different last names.

generations of well-known rabbis, Beider could trace his origins back to the end of the sixteenth century, to Rabbi Yehuda Loewe of Prague. Better known as the Maharal,[6] Rabbi Loewe was a scholar of Jewish philosophy and mysticism. He was immortalized by legend as the creator of the Golem of Prague, a mythical monster made of clay collected from the banks of the Vltava River and brought to life through rituals and Hebrew incantations.

In 1910 Rabbi Pearlmutter was appointed as the *Berezener*[7] Rabbi in Trochenbrod, and his family of seven children relocated. His two youngest sons were born there.

Much of Yisrael's early childhood was spent, however, in the town of Verba, studying Jewish tracts and scriptures with his grandfather Rabbi Zvi Hirsch. In later years he attended various *yeshivas*[8] including the famous Volozhin Yeshiva in Belarus. His deep knowledge of Jewish scriptures, literature, and traditions as well as the perfect mastery of Hebrew and Yiddish deeply influenced his literary work.

Although raised by his grandfather to follow in his ancestors' footsteps as a rabbi, Yisrael chose to become a schoolteacher instead. Like many of his contemporaries, he was attracted by the new culture of the twentieth century, which in the Jewish world was expressed by the revival of Hebrew,

---

6 מהר״ל, The acronym of the Hebrew words מורנו הרב ליווא (Moreinu ha-Rav Loewe, or Our Teacher Rabbi Loewe).
7 A stream of Khasidic Judaism that originated in Berezene, a town approximately sixty miles East of Trochenbrod.
8 Traditional Jewish learning establishment.

largely in the form of secular Hebrew[9] and the growth of the Zionist movement. His letters to his brothers placed him as a teacher in Olyka and Międzyrzecz, but for a certain time he also maintained a home in Trochenbrod. In his poem "In the Village" he talks about his return to his childhood home to visit his ancestral graves and describes his father's home:

> Father's home! Like a baby on his mom's arm
> with his mouth at her breast
> So did it cling lovingly to the *Beit Midrash*
> sucking the glow of its holy glory.
> Melancholic chants of pleas of repentance or
> the joyous sounds of studies late night,
> And at times the devotees' exhilaration when
> dancing to celebrate a joy of *mitzvah*...[10]

Though never stating explicitly the town's name, the poem described the synagogue that stood on Trochenbrod's main (and only) street with their home next door.

Wednesday nights, soon after the children were asleep, dozens of Trochenbrod's traders and craftsmen traveled in a caravan of horse wagons down a forest trail to sell and buy at the Olyka fair on Thursday. As a young child, Beider loved to watch the crowd of men, horses and wagons full of locally

---

9   Often referred to as the *Haskalah* (Enlightenment) Hebrew. The Haskalah Hebrew distinguished itself by purism; i.e., restricting it only to words of biblical origin and flowery language. These two components are easily recognized in Beider's writing.
10 Reference to the *Mitzvah Tantz*—the Hassidic custom of the men dancing in front of the bride.

made produce, dairy, and leather goods gather in the darkness in front of his house, getting louder and louder until someone gave a signal and the convoy began moving towards Olyka, where the weekly market was held. After Beila, his mother, left the room, Yisrael would kneel on his bed and watch the show until the last horse wagon, its lanterns swaying, followed those before it down the Olyka trail.

After the Great War and the death of his father, Yisrael lived for a few years in Trochenbrod with his mother and siblings. Eventually he was offered a job as head of a large Jewish school in the Polish city of Międzyrzecz. This was a significant honor, one that arose from his growing reputation as a master of Jewish studies and the renewed Hebrew language, but the honor did not alter his circumstances of poverty that had shadowed him in Trochenbrod.

Three of Yisrael's brothers, Naftali, Hayim, and Shimon, emigrated to Brazil, most likely in the early 1920s. Many of their offspring have since moved to Israel and established a large family there.

His older sister, Sarah, and his brother Ya'akov Pearlmutter, emigrated to the United States, also before the holocaust. Sarah married and lived with her family in New York. Ya'akov was ordained and became a well-known and highly respected rabbi in Baltimore; he is the author of Darchei Noam[11] (Ways of Pleasantness) that fostered an inclusive form of orthodox Judaism.

Ya'akov had three children: Sarah, who dedicated her life to her family and her surrounding Jewish community, especially

---

11 The name derives from Prov. 3:17

the children, for whom her house was filled with games and laughter as the central place for neighborhood Jewish children to play; Marvin, an entrepreneur who was a pioneer inventor and promoter of digital printing systems; and Fishel, who was ordained a conservative rabbi, practiced in Toledo, and dedicated his life to Conservative Judaism, civil rights, and women's rights, including the ordination of women in the Conservative movement.

Yisrael's youngest brother, YomTov Hagai, immigrated to Palestine in 1932 and in 1938 immigrated to the US. Of the nine siblings, only Yisrael, his sister Shifra and his brother Zvi Hirsch remained in Ukraine along with their own families and their mother.

Although one of his brothers, Hayim, pleaded with Yisrael in a 1923 letter to join him in Brazil, Yisrael provided numerous reasons why he could not leave; not the least of which was his wife Zlatka who never left Trochenbrod and still lived there with their two toddlers.

In one of his letters, Yisrael wrote to his brother Shimon that in 1931 he spent a few months in a "*kibbutz*" near Warsaw. Probably a reference to one of the *Hachshara* ("training") camps where pioneers received training prior to their immigration to Palestine by living in a commune, kibbutz style. But in the same letter he also said that the immigration of his group was delayed by British restrictions of entry to Palestine. Beider never made it to Palestine.

After their father's death and the end of the Great War and the Russian-Polish war, Shifra, who remained in Ukraine, married, moved to her husband's hometown, in the nearby city of Rovno, where she gave birth to a son named Moshe

David. Zvi Hirsch was ordained and became a rabbi in a small town near Kiev. Shifra, her son, and Zvi Hirsch perished in the Holocaust. Family lore tells that Shifra's husband set out to move to Palestine with the idea of bringing his wife and children over once he was settled there, but he seems to have disappeared along the way and was never heard from again.

The collection left behind by Beider is a unique literary and historic gem. A few of his poems and essays were published in prominent Hebrew and Yiddish publications of the time like *Ha-Olam*,[12] the official publication of the Zionist movement, or *Ha-Tsefira*, one of the longest running Hebrew papers in Europe. His works ran alongside pieces by leaders of the Zionist movement like Yitzhak Ben Zvi, poets like Bialik,[13] and Tchernichovsky, or novelists like Kabak. Yet, Beider never achieved similar recognition.

The present collection consists of forty-two poems (including a eulogy for his brother Shimon that was embedded in one of his letters), eight essays, and eight letters. The poems were grouped in this collection into the following categories according to their topic: Nature; the land of Israel; Family; Oppression; Old age; and Miscellaneous.

Of the pieces that were clearly dated, the earliest work is from 1923 and the latest is from 1939. While it is quite likely that Beider continued to produce until his death in 1942, we could not locate any of his later work. Search through

---

12 *Ha-Olam*, the central organ of the World Zionist Organization, was published as a weekly from 1907 to 1950 (except for short intervals).
13 Hayim Nahman Bialik (Jan. 9, 1873–July 4, 1934) was a Jewish poet often considered Israel's national poet.

the archives of the National Library of Israel, YIVO, and the Center of Jewish History in New York revealed only one additional poem in Yiddish that was translated and added to the present collection. None of the surviving family members could recall having any of Beider's writings.

We do not know how Beider's youngest brother YomTov Hagai obtained and saved this collection; he might have stopped in Trochenbrod on his way in 1938 from Palestine to the United States and collected it there. He never spoke about this collection, and after his death his son, Avrom Bendavid-Val, found it among his possessions. Realizing the importance of this material, he scanned it and donated some or all the originals to the US Holocaust Memorial Museum. Approximately half of the pages can be seen on the Museum's web site.[14] Apparently the originals of the remaining pieces that were translated and included in this collection were lost.

It is not known how much of Beider's work was ever considered for publication by contemporary papers. In one of his letters to his brother Hayim,[15] he stated that the cost of postage was beyond his means and precluded him from sending his work for review. We believe that much of his work was never published and that this translated collection is the most comprehensive assembly of his surviving writings.

---

14 See: https://collections.ushmm.org/search/catalog/irn84486?rsc=21919&cv=0&x=799&y=535&z=2.1e-4.
15 Hayim Shlomo Zalman. A family tree (see Appendix B) shows him as the fifth of nine siblings, with Yisrael being the second. Hayim, along with three other brothers moved to Brazil. August 28, 1923.

Trochenbrod, the Town That Was

By Avrom Bendavid-Val and Gabriel Laufer[1]

Trochenbrod, my father YomTov Hagai used to tell me, was a little town where everyone was a farmer and no one was a farmer. Early in the twentieth century, the town (along with the adjacent village Lozisht) counted approximately sixteen hundred people, but by the time it was invaded by the Nazis it had grown to about five thousand people. Trochenbrod was hidden deep in a forest in the Volyn province of Russia. After the Great War it became part of Poland and presently it is in the northwestern corner of Ukraine. We will refer to the town and its surrounding locations as Ukraine.

Trochenbrod was unique in history as a full-fledged officially recognized town situated in the gentile world but built, populated, and self-governed exclusively by Jews. Trochenbrod thrived as a Jewish town until its destruction

---

1   This article relies heavily on the book Avrom Bendavid-Val, *The Heavens Are Empty: Discovering the Lost Town of Trochenbrod* (New York: Pegasus Books, 2010).

and complete annihilation by the Nazis and their Ukrainian collaborators during World War II.

To be sure, Trochenbrod had those *shtetl* qualities captured with warmth and appreciation by prominent Jewish artists like Sholem Aleichem and Mark Chagall. But because Trochenbrod was relatively isolated, and because the people of Trochenbrod were farmers as well as shopkeepers and tradesmen those shtetl qualities were undiluted, magnified, and connected with the outdoors and a farming way of life unknown in other shtetls. It brought about a relaxed Jewish atmosphere where the Sabbath, Jewish holidays, and weddings were celebrated not just in town, but by the entire town.

This unique character was captured in the musical Fiddler on the Roof that was based on Sholem Aleichem's story "Tevye the Dairyman." Some claim that Sholem Aleichem actually visited Trochenbrod anonymously for inspiration. Without a doubt, much of Beider's work reflected his close interaction with nature in a remote agrarian village, like the lines from his poem "Under the Crescent Moon":

> The village slumbers
> Amid the woods,
> I am still awake
> Beneath the crescent moon.
>
> The brook too
> Never reposes—
> Crescent and I
> On its ripples we float.

Trochenbrod was originally settled in 1803 by Jewish risk-takers from nearby cities determined to escape the notice of Russian officials, and the oppressive measures by the Tsarist government, by undertaking farming on unused land. The Jews knew nothing about farming, and chances were that the unused land was the least suitable for farming. Yet oppressive decrees made Jews want to stay as far away as possible from the Tsarist government. Rural areas were the best place for that.

The early settlement was in a marshy clearing surrounded by dense pine forests in an area between the cities of Lutsk, Rovno, and Kolky. The land was the property of a local landholder named Trochin who was no doubt happy to let the Jewish settlers try to extract value from the otherwise useless property. A creek tumbled out of the forest and ran through the clearing before disappearing into the woods again. There was a shallow spot where travelers on a trail connecting villages in the area would ford the creek. The place was known as Trochin Ford. The word for ford in Russian is *brod*. To the Yiddish-speaking settlers, *Trochin Brod* eventually became Trochenbrod.[2] The first baby was born in Trochenbrod in 1813.

In his poem "The Village," Beider describes those early years:

---

2   Other accounts suggest that the name came from the Yiddish words *troken* (dry) and *broyt* (bread).

> Although they [our fathers and ancestors] too did not see happiness.[3]
> And for the stale bread their land provided
> They worked by the sweat of their brows in harsh labor.
> Even the pioneers who cleared the woods,
> And fought snakes and prairie wolves,
> Until they turned those primeval forests
> and ancient swamps into settlements and their homes,
> They too did not taste life's bitterness like us.

In the mid-1820s, a group of twenty-one Mennonite families left their village of Sofiyovka, seventy miles north-east of Trochenbrod, on the Horyn River, and established two small new settlements on land they deemed to be more fertile. One settlement, Yosefin, was set up three miles west of Trochenbrod. The other, just south of Trochenbrod, was named Sofiyovka after their old village.

About ten years later they abandoned their two new villages to join relatives in a larger Mennonite settlement in the Southern "New Russia" region.[4] Yosefin was repopulated by ethnic German families.

About that time Trochenbrod elders and the Russian government agreed that Trochenbrod would be given the status of an official colony. No one knows exactly why, but when the

---

3   From Job 9:25.
4   Today's southern Ukraine.

new colony first appeared on official maps it was given the name of the abandoned Mennonite village Sofiyovka. From then on, the village and later the town was known as both Trochenbrod and Sofiyovka.

After a few years on the land, with only mixed results to show for their efforts, the Trochenbroders began to augment work on their small farms with trades they had practiced in the cities. Over the next couple of decades, the farming settlement became a town of produce traders, workshops, tradesmen, shopkeepers, dairies, mills, and leather workers. Each family also cultivated a small plot behind their house, and many raised a few cows.

Though it never featured a regional weekly market, in due course Trochenbrod became a commercial center, a regional hub of sorts, for the surrounding farming villages, from which people reached it by horse and horse wagon through forest trails. It remained relatively unknown in the world beyond the forest that engulfed it. From the first settlers, everyone living in Trochenbrod was Jewish; they practiced their Jewish ways openly and proudly. Trochenbrod, where everyone was a farmer and no one was a farmer, was tight knit, like one large Jewish family.

The Beider house in Trochenbrod was located at the south end of town, next to the Berezner synagogue where the Berezner rabbi, Yisrael's father, had his study and where he spent most of his day.

Trochenbrod's houses were typical of the agrarian Ukrainian style: rectangular, dirt floors, wood framed stucco walls that were whitewashed, thatched roofs that sloped towards the long side of the houses, and often window frames with carved wood patterns that stood out quaintly against the stucco walls. In "The Village," Beider describes his father home:

> The whitewashed walls faded, a shade of blue now to their plain white,
> Paltiel the plasterer, blind in one eye, expert in mixing colors
> And singing "Dror Yikra"[5] in Wulach[6] tipsy style during the third meal,[7]
> Artfully and skillfully painted the walls in early spring year after year.
> A straight blue line he drew a smidgen under the roof to frame the wall,
> And miracle of miracles, bless Palti's one eye, the line was straight time after time.

The single street that ran the length of Trochenbrod was little more than a broad muddy path. To drain the street as well as possible, the townspeople dug drainage ditches along its sides and laid planks across the ditches to make bridges to their homes. The early settlers soon began planting willow trees along the street. For the generations that followed those trees lining the street were a prominent part of the image of Trochenbrod.

---

5 "He will proclaim freedom," a *piyyut*, a Jewish religious song traditionally sung during Shabbat meals.
6 Expressing an elegiac mood.
7 One is obligated to have three meals on Shabbat, one in the morning, one in the afternoon, and one in the evening.

To this day the trail that once was Trochenbrod's main street remains marked by a double row of willow trees and bushes. Beider in his poem "The Village" also recalled those willows:

> It [his childhood home] is paltry and modest
> from the outside as if infused by the spirits of
> its denizens
> Flower beds did not grace its small front yard
> nor a fruiting tree
> A meager young willow with barely a crown
> never put down roots,
> Symbolizing the family that came from afar to
> live in the Polesian lowland—[8]
> sat by the door sad, longing for waters of
> distant rivulets—

At its south end, just beyond the last house, Trochenbrod's main street split into a fork of two horse trails. One of the two, the Olyka trail disappeared into the sandy Radziwill forest south of Trochenbrod, and after twelve miles arrived at the town of Olyka, where a large market fair was held every week. Wednesday nights, soon after the children were asleep, dozens of Trochenbrod's traders and craftsmen traveled in a caravan of horse wagons down this trail to sell and buy at the Olyka fair on Thursday.

---

8 A vast area in the western portion of East Europe, stretching through Poland, Ukraine, and Belarus.

From the 1880s through the 1930s, except during WWI, Trochenbrod sent waves of immigrants to North and South America, and between the wars to Palestine as well. Three of Beider's siblings ended up in Brazil, two in the US and one (YomTov Hagai) in Palestine.[9]

For many Trochenbroders, especially young men, there were many reasons for emigrating. Stories of unbelievable economic opportunities in America were a strong draw, while physical expansion to accommodate the children of Trochenbrod families was not possible because the town was hemmed in by forests owned by wealthy Polish gentry who were profiting nicely from the timber produced by that forest. Though Trochenbrod's relative isolation shielded it from anti-Jewish hooligans so far, reports of pogroms and antisemitic attacks across Russia suggested trouble ahead.

This too factored into Beider's work as reflected in his Yiddish poem "On the Water":[10]

> My brothers reached the longed-for shore,
> Landed on a solid land,
> Only I remained on the water, caught in midstream,
> My ship is fully loaded with heavy freight.
>
> I was late, that is; I was sure to catch up,
> In the meantime, night suddenly fell,
> And who knows how long until day?
> My terrain is foamy sea, dark skies cover me.

---

9 YomTov Hagai immigrated from Palestine to the US in 1938.
10 Published in the *Mezryczer Trybune*, issue 39 (October 6, 1930), 3.

In the early twentieth century, as the world moved inexorably toward World War I and Russia toward the Bolshevik Revolution, ideological currents coursing through Europe began to seep into Trochenbrod. Communist, Labor Zionist, Beitar (a right-leaning Zionist youth organization that stressed self-defense), General Zionists, and other secular movements sprouted in the town. Trochenbrod became somewhat more contemporary, with a wide assortment of religious, cultural, and social organizations, and an ever-expanding array of businesses. By the time WWI erupted, many Trochenbroders were regularly visiting the nearby cities for trade, medical attention, government affairs, or to visit relatives. The town continued to prosper and diversify in terms of the numbers and variety of economic activities.

World War I brought devastation and hardship to Trochenbrod, as it did to most of Europe. As the front between the Habsburg Austrian troops and Russian troops shifted back and forth through the area around Trochenbrod, there was intense fighting and widespread destruction in the town itself. A glass factory in town along with several other factories were destroyed, livestock were confiscated, homes and shops looted, and remittance from relatives abroad stopped arriving.

Following the Great War, Russia and Poland fought over who would rule a large area that included Trochenbrod. Again, the front moved back and forth through the area. Again, Trochenbrod was ravaged, and suddenly, after being a Russian town for more than a century, Trochenbrod became Polish.

The first few years after the war were a period of harsh life and recovery. In the early years of full Polish administration, local commandants imposed forced labor on the Jews of Trochenbrod—building roads, administration buildings and warehouses in the region; supplying the Polish army with food, clothes, and leather goods; hauling construction material and army supplies; building furnishing for government offices.

Beider describes this hardship in his poem "From the Abyss":[11]

> At dawn on Shabbat armed Cossacks appeared,
> > Each one with a crop in hand
> > And serpent's venom in his heart,
> To round up Jews for labor in the "city's defense."
>
> Lurking since yesterday were: piles of barbed wires,
> > Poles, stakes and tools for the workers,
> > Hatchets and axes all ready for battle—
> To build iron walls and levies on the River Styr's[12] banks.
>
> > > ***
> > > ***
> > > ***
>
> But one refused stubbornly to desecrate the Shabbat,
> > The son of a rabbinic creed.
> > Short, weak, and meager face,

---

11 Published in *Ha-Olam*, issue 41 (October 20, 1931), 825.
12 The river flowing through Lutsk, the city nearest to Trochenbrod.

His heroic heart turned courageous by the fear
and love of the creator.

And his soul became a vessel for the swearing
and cursing his flesh to vicious thrashings:
> Beaten by the rod and shoved,
>> Thrown around like a ball and dragged,
But he took it lovingly like the innocent saints
did.

That hardship was soon replaced with higher-level official discrimination. Government jobs were denied to Jews. Some trades that Jews had been prominent in, such as vodka and salt, were monopolized by the state and turned over to Polish Catholic war veterans. Systemic repression of Jews steadily increased throughout the interwar period.

World War I and the Polish-Soviet war transformed Trochenbrod into a new Trochenbrod. The old Trochenbrod was insular: the only thing that had been important to most people was Jewish law, traditions, and holy books. Reading was limited to the Torah and its commentaries and rabbinic tracts. Only the Jewish holidays were observed. And the Sabbath was observed strictly.

During the wars, Trochenbrod rubbed up against soldiers—Russian, Austrian, Soviet, Polish. Some young men had run off to far-away cities to avoid the invaders, and after the wars, returned more world-wise. Some had been taken into the army by one side or the other and forced to live in a gentile world without kosher food. After the wars many of Trochenbrod's young men cut off their side-curls and even smoked shamelessly on the Sabbath; newspapers came regularly to the town; the Polish government established a public school, and even paved a section of Trochenbrod's main street with stones to make it passable after rain. Zionist political organizations from right to left arose, and most young people belonged to them; gasoline powered motors were brought in to run the rebuilt flour mills and oil presses; Trochenbroders began to travel more often to Lutsk, Rovno, Kolky, and even further afield. Trochenbrod was still mostly secluded, but its people came to internalize much more than before that there was an outside world that mattered, a large outside world with a vast variety of people and countries; younger Trochenbroders liked that.

This is not to overstate the case. Trochenbrod remained surrounded by forests, far from any reliable transportation route for motorized vehicles and somewhat insular and Jewish. It remained a town governed exclusively by Jewish customs; always observing the Sabbath and Jewish holidays and always greeting visiting Jewish scholars with celebration. For Jews who knew about the town and for most who lived there, this together with the farming character, lent Trochenbrod an out-of-place and out-of-time almost magical quality.

As the 1920s gave way to the 1930s, Trochenbrod was thriving again. Its economy was increasingly becoming dependent on trade, artisans, agroprocessing, and light manufacturing for a region stretching in a radius of about ten miles. Much has been made, and rightly so, of the uniqueness of Trochenbrod's Jewish farmers at that time.

Although everyone worked their land to some degree, the livelihoods of most Trochenbrod families now came from retail shops, leather related businesses, construction trades, small-scale manufacturing, and trading.

Trochenbrod's economic expansion, diversification, and extension of its market reach continued at a brisk pace until late 1939, bringing with it more than tripling of its population from sixteen hundred to over five thousand in Trochenbrod and Lozisht combined.

Some of that population growth resulted from people moving to Trochenbrod from surrounding cities, by marriage, or because it was a uniquely desirable place for Jews. Some of the growth was caused by reduced migration out of town, largely because Jews were denied entry to other countries. And some of the growth could be attributed to higher birth rates spurred by economic recovery.

In October 1939, Trochenbrod came under Soviet rule once again. This was the consequence of the Molotov-Ribbentrop pact of non-aggression between Germany and the Soviet Union, which in fact partitioned Poland between the two countries. As soon as the Soviets took control of Trochenbrod, local Jewish communists were installed as mayor, police, and other local officials. The Polish post office was closed. The Soviets took over much of the economic property in Trochenbrod—small factories, workshops, even some shops. Typically, they put the workers in charge and turned the owners into workers. Most family enterprises that did not employ workers were allowed to continue operating as before, but some were taken over by upper-level communists "for the people." People were driven into poverty while shortages were developing. Food was rationed through a cooperative store. People hid property, including their own stock of food. Consequently, a black market developed even for basic necessities. People had little money, but there was little to buy.

The Soviets were not particularly anti-Jewish and allowed the language of instruction in Trochenbrod schools to remain Yiddish, though all students also had to study Russian. Consistent with Soviet ideology, the Soviets strongly discouraged religious observance. They interfered with synagogue prayers and tried to impose labor on Sabbath. But in the end, because on a day-to-day basis matters were run mostly by local people, there were often ways to circumvent Communist doctrine and maintain Jewish life and culture reasonably well.

However difficult was the life under the Soviet regime, it came to an end too soon. When the Germans invaded Soviet-held lands on June 22, 1941, Trochenbrod and its sister village Lozisht had a combined population of six thousand Jews. Within days, the Germans marked Trochenbrod's houses with Jewish stars, murdered citizens randomly and invited destruction and looting of Jewish possessions by encouraging rampaging Ukrainian villagers that were now freed from the restraints by the departing Soviets. They set up a local administrative system, the *Judenrat* or Jewish council, to carry out German orders such as providing Jews for forced labor or collecting "taxes." The German administration system also included auxiliary police and a Ukrainian militia to police the Jews, hunt them down when they tried to escape the terror, and eventually assist in their liquidation.

The Ukrainian militia's aim was to purify Ukraine by ridding it of Jews, Poles, Russians, and ultimately Germans, and fulfill an old dream of an independent and "pure" Ukraine. People from nearby villages with whom Trochenbroders had close relationships turned into collaborators with the Nazi regime and treated their Trochenbrod neighbors with cruelty and brutality.

By the spring of 1942, it became increasingly clear to many Trochenbroders that the Germans intended to ultimately kill them all: either by exploiting them as slave labor, starvation, or by outright murder. Some built false walls in their houses or farms as hiding places; some prepared bunkers in the forest; some found false identity papers and began to slip away; and some young men fled into the forest and started training to become partisans. But most still clung to the hope that their utility to the Germans would protect them. They struggled to survive heavier and heavier despair while awaiting their fate.

As elsewhere, the Nazi murder machine was very organized and methodical. Their plan called for a schedule of exterminations that would leave Ukraine "Judenfrei"[13] by October 10, 1942. Accordingly, most of the Jews of Kolky were slaughtered on August 9, most of Olyka's Jews on August 10. The Jews of Trochenbrod were scheduled to be slaughtered on August 11.

On the morning of Sunday, August 9, 1942, twenty soldiers of the Einsatzgruppe C.—one of Germany's death squads, rode into town on motorcycles, followed by eleven German army trucks carrying a hundred Ukrainian militia men. After rounding up all Trochenbrod's people at the center of the town, they notified them that as of that moment that area was the Jewish ghetto, and all must remain within its boundaries. Fifty leather workers and their families whose skills were needed at

---

13 In German, free of Jews.

the time by the Germans were exempted and ordered to move to a cluster of houses north of town.

On the morning of August 11, Trochenbrod's Jews were called out of the ghetto houses and were ordered to prepare for transport and that they should bring food for three days. They were loaded into trucks and taken, two hundred at a time, to the killing pits in the Yaromel' forest, about two miles out of town, that the Ukrainian militia men had dug several days earlier.

The Jews were ordered off the trucks that were stopped near the pits. Once they reached the pits the Germans ordered them to undress and shot them letting their naked bodies collapse into the pits on top of their neighbors who were shot before.

Each new group saw clearly what happened to those who came before. Many became hysterical and some jumped a guardsman and screamed for everyone to run. Some indeed bolted. Most were shot, but a few managed to escape into the forest. Their deaths were merely delayed. They were hunted by everyone: Germans, militia men, and ordinary villagers, who usually cut them down.

Late that afternoon the *Aktion*[14] was over. The trucks made their final trip back to Trochenbrod carrying the victims' clothing and other valuables.

Forty-five hundred Jews from Trochenbrod and Lozisht were murdered on that day. More than three thousand additional Jews from Trochenbrod-Lozisht and their surroundings were murdered in the following weeks and months.

---

14 In German, military operation.

Approximately five hundred to one thousand people remained alive in the Trochenbrod ghetto. Some escaped into the forest but most returned when they realized that they could not survive there. More were transferred to the ghetto from the surrounding area until ultimately the population grew to about fifteen hundred.

Yom Kippur, the Day of Atonement, fell that year on September 21. As the date drew closer, more and more people came in from the forest to spend what they knew was likely to be their last Yom Kippur, praying with their Trochenbrod friends and relatives. About two weeks earlier, thirty of the leather workers were marched to the Yaromel' forest to dig a second set of mass graves near the first graves. While digging, one of them, reportedly the tanner Moshe Shwartz, suddenly rose up and attacked three of the guards with his shovel while screaming to the others to save themselves. Many began to flee into the forest, but most of them, like Moshe Shwartz, were killed by German and Ukrainian gunfire.

On Yom Kippur the second Aktion was completed: almost everyone in the Trochenbrod ghetto was taken to the second set of pits and slaughtered like the first group six weeks earlier. Still, a few somehow remained alive.

In December, all remaining Jews were taken to the pits and shot. To mark completion of Trochenbrod's eradication, the Nazis set fire to the synagogue. That spot is marked today by a modest black marble monument.

We do not know if Yisrael Beider and his two sons[15] were among Trochenbrod's victims or whether they found their

---

15   His wife Zlata, to whom he referred with the affectionate "Zlatka," died in 1931 of a long disease.

deaths elsewhere. But we do know that they, along with his sister Shifra and her children and his brother Zvi Hirsch perished in the Holocaust.

May their memory be a blessing.

Many of Trochenbrod's houses disappeared soon after. The Germans demanded at least one laborer from every household in the surrounding villages for five days to work on dismantling many of Trochenbrod's houses and other buildings. All remaining furniture was removed from the houses and then the buildings were disassembled into building materials. Clothes and furniture were sold to local villagers. Some of the building material was used for military construction, and the rest was loaded on trucks and taken to Kivertzy for shipment to Germany to offset shortages there. Later, partisans set fire to the houses that were left to deny their use to the Germans and their Ukrainian collaborators. After the Germans were driven out by the Red Army in 1944, Ukrainians from surrounding villages took anything remaining that could be moved, including the paving stones from Trochenbrod's streets.

Trochenbrod had vanished.

Of the more than six thousand people in Trochenbrod and Lozisht at the time of the Nazi invasion, possibly sixty survived. These were people that retreated with the Soviets or escaped later across the Soviet border; or people who obtained false documents.

Acknowledgements

The translation of this collection would not have been possible without Susan (Suzy) Goldstein Snyder, a curator at the Curatorial Affairs Branch, David M. Rubenstein National Institute for Holocaust Documentation. I am a volunteer translator for the museum and it was up to her to introduce me to the most unique and interesting documents in the archive that needed to be translated from Hebrew. She did so before and did it again. I am grateful to her for the privilege of translating this collection of poems, essays, and letters.

Equally so, I am indebted to the late Avrom Bendavid-Val, one of the many nephews of Yisrael Beider. Avrom distinguished himself through his life in many ways, including by becoming one of the stewards of the story of Trochenbrod. In addition to his unique insight into the history of this lost town and Beider's brief life, he had in his possession additional writings by Beider which he generously shared with me. Avrom was also uniquely helpful in editing this work and contributing to the introductory material.

Some of Beider's writings were in Yiddish. Thanks to the generous commitment and skillful translation by Andrew Cassel and Ellen Cassedy, those writings could also be included in this collection.

Translating text written in what is known as Haskalah Hebrew is challenging by itself. However, translating poetry is doubly so. I tried to preserve the poetic beauty of Beider's writings. But ultimately, I had to rely on the talent of a true poet. Thanks to Professor Ellen Kronowitz who reviewed and edited the translated poems, much of their poetic qualities were preserved while also retaining the translation accuracy.

It is not often that the artwork of a book is contributed by an excellent artist who is also personally connected to the book's theme. As an award-winning graphic designer and a descendant of Trochenbrod survivors Andrea Liss was the natural choice to illustrate this book's cover. I am grateful for her wonderful and imaginative artwork.

Last but not least, I would like to acknowledge Marvin Bendavid's generous support that helped bring this collection to print.

Notes on the Text

Admittedly, no translation can fully convey the nuances and flavors of an original, particularly that of poetry. This one is especially vulnerable, both because of Beider's unusual literary style but also because the English version is the work of an interested volunteer rather than a trained scholar or linguist. I hope that this translation can still do justice to an otherwise extraordinary work.

Beider's literary style—a product of his traditional childhood and yeshiva education—makes extensive use of phrases and expressions drawn from biblical, Talmudic, and other rabbinic writings. Wherever possible, these sources were referenced by footnotes, along with other terms such as geographic locations, events, historic facts, and personalities. The translation of biblical quotes was standardized by using www.sefaria.org, where the Contemporary Torah, JPS, 2006 version is being used.

Often the footnotes relate to a fraction of a sentence, or even a single word that is not in daily use. Consequently, that footnote's number was placed by the actual quote rather than the end of the sentence in which it was included.

Names of geographical locations were spelled using their current spelling.

An effort was made to preserve in translation the literary beauty and accuracy of the poems, their structure and layout. Consequently, a few verses in some of the poems do not meet rigorous grammatical formats. Similarly, the punctuation used by Beider in his poems was replicated here even if it did not meet English standards. The layout of the poems is not uniform but it too replicates their original format. Hopefully the reader will be able to look beyond these deficiencies.

On occasion, a word or a sentence was not clear or required further clarification. On those instances I added a comment, or a question mark, and enclosed it in square parentheses [ ].

1

POEMS

Nature

A Winter Poem[1]

B[2]

When the blizzard blows
Flowers of snow—
My heart yearns for
Homeland blossoms.

    When clouds block
    The cold sun—
    My heart yearns for
    Warm, unclouded land.

        When the frost freezes
        The creek's murky waters—
        My heart yearns for the land
        Where dew is reviving

---

1 Courtesy of the United States Holocaust Memorial Museum—The Israel Beider collection. Although Beider's first name is spelled "Yisrael" in this book, it is spelled by the USHMM as "Israel." For the sake of consistency this latter spelling was used when referring to the USHMM collection.
2 This poem is labelled "B" (and the following three poems are likewise lettered) because it is the second in a series of five poems; "When the Eighth Candle Dies Out" was labeled as the first poem but owing to its content it was put in the later section "Oppression."

From the Valley[3]

C

Towering-peaks
Support the sky:
They watch all
In the distance.

From the valleys
Among graves,
I turn my eyes
To the mountains.[4]

Dwellers on high
The giants, I implore
Please save me
Dweller of depths

---

3   Courtesy of the United States Holocaust Memorial Museum—The Israel Beider collection. Previously published in *Ha-Tsefira*, Issue 77 (March 30, 1928), 3.
4   Ps. 121:1.

Fearing death[5]
Here below—
Raise me from
The deep pit.[6]

Mute they stand there
The mountains;
Watching over all below—
But forever from above...

---

5   Ps. 55:5.
6   Ps. 7:16.

Cloudlets[7]

D

Every morning[8] new
Cloudlets are born
Gentle, afloat—
Astonishing the eye.[9]

All crimson,
In the morning breeze
They glow and flutter
Pure and bright.

At times they
Hide the skyline,
Light like fluff,
Scales of clouds.

Some remind me
Of giant mushrooms
Or oaks soaring
In the azure sky.

Or maybe knights
Displaying their might
Riding on the lofts[10]
Of showoff clouds.

And I may imagine:
Cherubs and angels there
Spreading silvery wings
And flying away.

Many and varied are
The cloudlets' colors,
To me they are all lovely,
Delicate and delightful.

II

In prayer to the cloudlets
I will silently raise my arms:
Grant me one small drop
As an offering from above.

---

7 Courtesy of the United States Holocaust Memorial Museum—The Israel Beider collection. The title comes from a rarely used word, derived from a similar Talmudic expressions "מעבב."
8 A Talmudic expression.
9 A Talmudic expression.
10 Term from 2 Sam. 1:19.

It would be to my eyes
An eternal comforting tear,
To relieve my sorrow
Lessen my pain just a bit.

That little drop would
Heal an aching heart,
Calm my wounds
Until my pain is gone.

Because your crown is pure
Steeped in radiance
Elevated and detached
From this land below.

Bless me Cloudlets
With one droplet of pureness,
Shed from your richness
A little blessing to the poor.

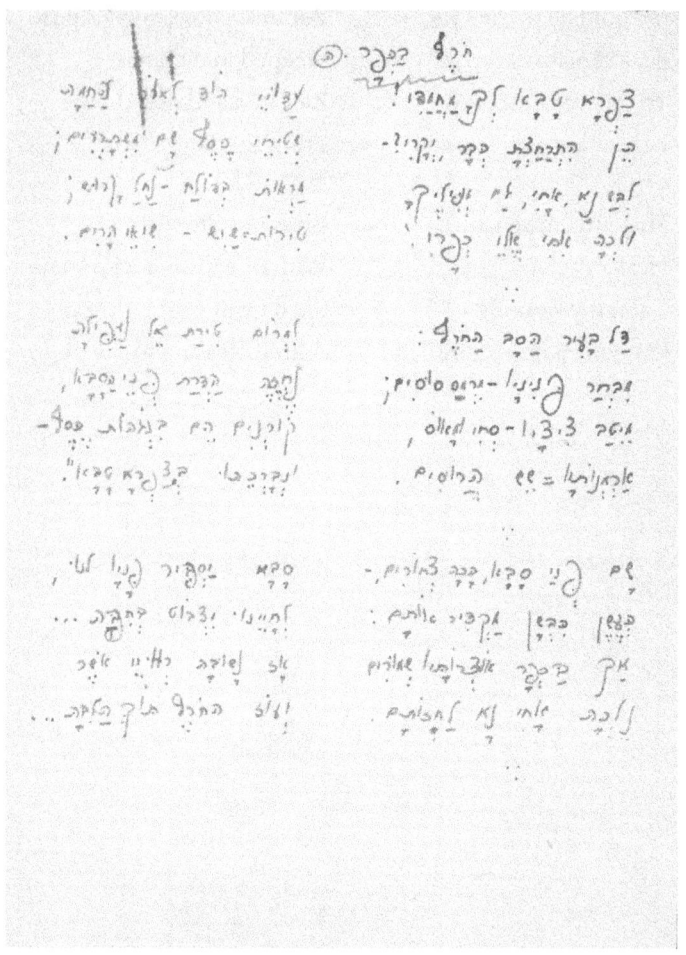

Winter in the Countryside. Image of the handwritten original of the poem "Winter in the Countryside." Courtesy of the United States Holocaust Memorial Museum—The Israel Beider collection.

Winter in the Countryside[11]

E

Good morning[12] to you my adored beloved!
Did you already bathe my dear sibling?
Put on your coat, my brother,
And come with me to my village!

Old man winter is feeble in the city:
The best of its treasures—trampled by horses;
The best of its gems—filthy with refuse;
Its alabaster[13] palaces—are in ruins.

There old man's[14] face should be pale,
And furnace smoke blackens it:
In the countryside its treasures are preserved
Let's go out my brother to see them.

Majestically dressed at sunlight
Silvery carpets stretch out far;
Frozen rivers are like crystal mirrors;
Mountain peaks like marble castles.

---

11 Courtesy of the United States Holocaust Memorial Museum—The Israel Beider collection.
12 From Aramaic.
13 Term used in Esther 1:6.
14 Reference to winter.

Let us scale the top of the divine castle
To witness old-man-winter's brilliance
Radiating in glistening glow—
And wish him "a good cockcrow."

Old man winter will smile at us,
And pinch our cheeks lovingly . . .
Then we'll head back full of joy
With winter's might in our core . . .

Here worry, sorrow and pain are ignored
The air here heals the soul and body.
Leave behind your remote corner in the city
Hasten to the country brother, please!

On the Farm[15]

Lead skies weigh down
On the farm all daylong.
A flying crow shrieks from above
"Fall has arrived" she cries.

Robbed of its gold the wheat field
Appears solemn, mournful.
My flower bed's fragrance
Faded, withered, and wilted.

And the creek, all furrowed,
Like an enraged old man:
The whole universe deathly ill[16]
Its moans—horrifying.

---

15 Courtesy of the United States Holocaust Memorial Museum—The Israel Beider collection. Previously published in *Ba-Derekh*, issue 9 (November 10, 1932), 5.
16 A Talmudic expression, e.g., Gittin 73a:2.

Frost[17]

There are trees in my garden whose buds froze in the frost;
Their limbs, trunks and roots decimated by the long winter's cold...
When the garden's trees bear fruit again as the cold days come to an end,
These trees will remain barren looking sickly and gloomy:

Soon the golden spring sun will germinate a bouquet of flowers—
Exposing the nakedness of the dead limbs for all to see
Suddenly the whistling wings will drift away from thee,
To nest in the shelter of thick twigs
And cast from there merry chirps.

And the new wind, will soar to announce the new rebirth,
That a new age is back in the world
And the creation's youth is restored—
Quickly truncating the meager and exposed limbs,
Separating and tossing to earth crowns from detached bodies,
Leaving them and dashing to the depth of their boughs

Kiss the new buds and bless their sweet perfume.
Dew of new life will quench all the plants on fertile earth—
And the leafless will shed tears for the sadness of the terrible frost,
Like condemned they will wait silently for their certain death,
Until a strike of a saw will turn them into briers and thistles...[18]

---

17   From the collection of Avrom Bendavid-Val.
18   Isa. 5:6.

Between Trickles[19]

Between one trickle and another
The clouds dissipate.
The heavens clear
Beautiful and enchanting

A cheerful sun
Shows a friendly face
Such a pleasant smile—
Dandyish youth.

Brother, don't allow
Yourself to be deluded
Never trust
The Autumn's sun.

Spring is long gone
Never returning
Now is Fall's turn
Violent and harsh

Don't trust the smile
It fades in an instant,
Skies darken again,
The trickle now is rain . . .

---

19   From the collection of Avrom Bendavid-Val.

A Note from the Countryside[20]

Shalom my brother endless blessings!
So said your brother. Hasten to me!
Leave behind your tiny and damp cellar,
Jammed between suffocating city alleys.
Hurry to the wide spaces, spacious countryside
No shadows of tall fences and walls.
Come my brother, escape the crevices
Between remote alleys of your town . . .

Daylight has not died; it's still not dusk—
Hasten and give me your hand—
Golden glimmers of light still trick the fields;
Doves not yet asleep among tree branches;
Everything is so quiet, mystery in its shroud,
The aura of beauty hovers above -
Locked in each other's arms, we'll ascend the mountain,
To see the majesty of our countryside.

From there we'll see the beauty of its fields and woods;
Ornate with sprinkles of sunlight radiating in its glow;
Peaceful huts, sheltering homes,
Glorious blue skies majestically stretched above;
This meandering brook winding between peaks
Where little dinghies carry farmers to fish.

---

20 From the collection of Avrom Bendavid-Val.

Hurry my brother please come here.
We'll stroll quietly along the garden's groves
Even bathe in the pearl droplets of dew,
Drizzling at dawn from every treetop,
We'll dance like little lambs on grassy turf,
Climb like squirrels on trees and shrubs.

We'll roll along the mountain slope to the valley below,
Will play like little children once again.
Will be free here like the soaring birds,
Light and happy like beams of light . . . .
Here worry sorrow and pain all disappear,
The air here will cure your body and spirit.

Forsake brother your remote corner of town;
Rush to the country brother come!

Alone[21]

When my bare room gets too tight
To hold my silent sorrow
And would expel us both out—
My feet will transfer me running
To the vast open prairies,
At the foot of a mountain
That stands still and frozen
Like me with my burden.

Even if I don't reach its summit
That glows in the golden sun;
And if my head and heaven never meet
And my eyes at the horizon never stare—
My grief will be lessened in its shade
Hiking its golden sandy trail
Meditating, alone—on its slope.

But I would not walk along the other path:
To town, the market, its avenues,
At every street corner,[22] raucous crowds—
Everywhere trees grow only gloom;
Desecration behind every corner.
No place for a heartfelt prayer
From a lonely
Wanderer . . .

---

21 From the collection of Avrom Bendavid-Val.
22 Lam. 4:1.

Alien [country][23]

A

Please accept dear brother these greetings from afar
From a homeland so alien, in the Vale of Tears.[24]
    I know she has no name: Dear Motherland,
    She spit her sons like you out of their estates.
Her wealth and her bounty not to you were extended,
Her breast she never offered, a kiss to you never gave.
    Thirst consumed you, never satisfied—[25]
    For you, fiery serpents her bosom spawned,
Your essence poisoned with their rage and venom:
Only indignity you endured, affliction you silently bore
    In your waif's heart jealousy burned
    Seeing her own sons contently nurse.
I know it all, but ha! Also that I know,
She was your Motherland, here you were born.
    Her sun was the first light your eyes ever saw
    Her morning dew you suckled at your early dawn.
The gold of her breast, the dark of her woods you so yearn,
Are imprinted in your flesh in your heart forever burned.
    Her spring breeze caressed your locks
    Dabbed your sweat, renewed your strength.[26]

---

23 From the collection of Avrom Bendavid-Val.
24 From the 3rd stanza of *Lekha Dodi*, a traditional liturgical song recited at the start of the Friday night prayer, welcoming the Shabbat.
25 From Ps. 107:9.
26 From Ps. 19:8.

Your paradise she was in those old days.
That's where you walked like in a fairy land—
>But then you grew, matured as fruit, became a man
>Watching with your eyes her rebel sons[27] all around...

Pauper and confused, replete with disgrace...[28]
Like a captive from prison for your life you ran.
And now that you found—did you indeed find?
A loving homeland—to which you looked up,[29]
>Account to her favor the devotions of your youth[30]
>The beauty of her forests and her skies so blue.

Please accept my lovely brother the blessings I send
From the Valley of Baca,[31] a distant foreign land.

---

27 From Num. 17:25.
28 Job 10:15.
29 Gen. 18:2.
30 From Jer. 2:2.
31 Ps. 84:7.

On the Way to the Village[32]

B

Along the sandy trails that traverse,
Old forests in the plains,
Weaving among birch and oak,
Curving like a question mark,
> As if wondering, asking,
> Why would men and beast
> Disturb old oaks'
> Sleep and sweet dreams—

The wagon crawled, lethargic,
Groaning and screeching
Vigorously protesting,
Her weighty burden
> Of these two passengers
> Sitting atop bags of hay,
> On their way to family graves,
> In a hamlet on a land faraway.

The two passengers are forced
To suffer silently many jolts
For there are many roots
Curling under the bumpy road....
> Their heads submissively bowed
> As if curtsying and thanking
> The greetings sent down
> By the oak limbs stretching above.

---

32 From the collection of Avrom Bendavid-Val.

They like the silence those,
Who flee ear splitting fairs' noise,
To delight in tranquil sights
Mourn by serene gravesites.
> So nice and sweet the silence here,
> Along familiar childhood paths,
> Succumbing to the mind that revives
> The cloth of a glorious past.
Dredging up from submerged bottoms
Azure prairies of younger past ages,
Distilling out of the heavy fogs of years
Faces, images, and characters.
> It is pleasant to reflect along the road
> About that lovely native land—
> A village, a Jewish settlement,
> Surrounded by a forested wall that
Isolates and defends what it owns
From the bustle of markets:
Its vast fields and prairies
Skies extending to far horizons;
> Where poor Jews plow.
> These honest and innocent men,
> Quench their meager land
> By the sweat of their emaciated brows.[33]

---

33 Though Beider does not name the village, this and the previous two stanzas describe Trochenbrod as we know it from other publications (e.g., Ben David-Val, *The Heavens Are Empty: Discovering the Lost Town of Trochenbrod*).

The horses tread in the sands,
Slowly with expression of scorn
To the rush and haste
Of a mean world gone amok.
>	It seems there is no sense or insight,
>	In the minds of these lazy horses:
>	But in the quiet of virgin woods,
>	In the depth of a dark canyon,

Among giant conquering pines
In the silence of their lofty heights,
Amid their sturdy arms
Supporting the skies above:
>	On the road to ancestors' tombs
>	In that hidden distant village
>	That no car ever ran along its road
>	And no airplane ever flew above—

They might be right after all:
"Slow down man with thy hubris!
Don't let thy mad rush defile
Sanctity and glory of a world so nice!
>	Look around and watch
>	Tranquility and peace spread.
>	Beware of getting hurt
>	By this dizzying unrest . . .

People are dashing and rushing,
Crossing lands without stopping,
Flying across oceans like lightnings,
To the heights of heavens climbing:

> Millions of people are obsessed
> Giving up poetics and any sense
> To the gods of road haste—
> How terrible is that waste

Defiling a beauty so sacred
In the senseless packed race,
With no purpose, goal or end—
How boring, uninspiring and tame!

***   ***   ***

> I don't mind moving so slow,
> Or even if the dray came to a stop.
> I long, I yearn[34] for this temple my host,
> Where everything majestically grows!

How fair are your tents[35] my shrine!
Within lovely boulevards of your growth
Under the round crowns of treetops,
Painted gold by the rising sun above:

> Along sleepy dewy trails
> Padded with pine needles more than a few—
> How I loved getting
> lost there and sing
> Imitating birds nesting above on trees.

For the blood of my young heart hummed
Along with the plentiful army of vistas and sounds—
And tunes emerge out of my mouth
Like the harmony of flutes and violins.

---

34 From Ps. 84:3.
35 Num. 24:5.

> My heart was then fluttering
> Expecting sounds of fairies
> To join me in singing
> From shades and crannies ....

I loved wandering and searching
Among the riches of your shrine:
For pinecones and ant mounds,
Morrells, chestnuts, or nuts.

> But so much water passed under the bridge
> Sweeping away since those blessed days
> My childhood memories. All carried away,
> Into the seas of my salty tears.

Now I walk with my back bent
Under the burden of old events
Suffering for sins that weigh me down
My heart is like a stone-full bag—

> Wandering, empty handed and naked,
> I will pour out my heart on ancestors' graves
> The song of my life and its thunder are gone
> And the lovely fairies turned silent and mute ....

In the Village[36]

C

They did not rise from their depths; my suns are still set;[37]
My stars did not rekindle their sparkle that is long dead,
>> But in the spring when the snow melts
>> Last fall's rotten leaves are revealed—
Dancing flying in the blowing wind;
So is my tired quivering spirit trembling
>> At the village for the greetings
>> By my acquaintances of old days.
Here are my childhood pals, that
Played with me when my sun still smiled:
>> A few shrubs scattered around the grassland,
Bathed in twilight dew and dimming glow,
>> Of a tired meager setting sun—
>> Standing immobile like in prayer, still;
Dusty cows are pacing slowly,
Their udders heavy, back from the prairies
>> On trails stretching through bare fields
>> Resting peacefully in primordial majesty:
Wild grown pines and red berry shrubs
On the edges of azure and darkening groves;
>> How lovely it is to sit and listen to the hush
>> Or roast on a campfire a handful of spuds.

---

36 From the collection of Avrom Bendavid-Val.
37 From Gen. 15:17.

Watch the rising smoke, swirling on its way up,
Rising to the heavens thinning until gone . . .
> Or getting drenched by evening dew, pleasant and fun
> Like those innocent days of childhood long gone,

Or resign from the world, its clatter and its sounds,
Who stole my innocence and the grace of God. . . .
> And here are the gardens where corn and poppy grow,
> And string beans climbing along tall poles,

With vines, green leaves and many pods
Dangling like crystals from a candelabrum . . .
> And down there in the mournful swamp, flares
> And blazes scaring away the darkness off the plains.

And what is there striking a string in my heart?
Is that a miracle bringing back the spring of my past?
> Could these wonderful sights be no more than
> Imaginary lights that come and go late at night?

It is just the rot, my memories that rot,
Loves that turned ash, yearnings into dust.
> When a fading tinkle from a distant bell jingles,
> It brings back echoes of laughs and giggles.

A tiny relic still survives from my joy that once existed—
It still flutters but soon it too will be eradicated . . .
> Slowly the minister of the night descends,
> Opens a wide mouth for a big yawn,
> Traps the universe in its dark black maw,
> Swallows my few friends in its deep throat
> Silences the remaining echoes still in my soul.

The coachman stirred and woke from his light nap:
The horses sensed that soon is time for their respite—
They merrily sneezed and widened their pace.
We soon reached the village's edge,
Silently embraced in the darkness arms.

A red flicker in a window is alight,
Blinking like a swollen ailing eye—
Ugly, murky this little glint of light
Drizzling out of the wick of a sooty lamp
Like the synagogue's perpetual light.

But even a little glint is a wanderer's delight
Thirsting[38] for salvation from the hold of the dark...
It might even be better than electric light,
Full of cheerful vanity, conceit and pride,
Infesting filthy streets of cities and capitals.

The coachman rolled a "*Makhorka*"[39] cig
Striking a flint against steel he shot sparks
That rushed like angry flies into the dark
The smoke streamed through the words of his yak,
Apparently easing the burden of his long hush.

So what, friends, is going in the vast world?
Is life in the big cities also that hard?
Like here in this remote part?

---

38   From Ps. 63:2.
39   Cheap tobacco smoked in Russia and neighboring countries.

Ah bad times arrived—not seen like these even by
Our fathers and their ancestors in their dreams.
Although they too did not see happiness.[40]
And for the stale bread their land provided
They worked by the sweat of their brows in harsh labor.
Even the pioneers who cleared the woods,
And fought snakes and prairie wolves,
Until they turned those primeval forests
and ancient swamps into settlements and their homes,
They too did not taste life's bitterness like us.

The neglected as if abandoned small town
Not a guard or police within its boundary.
Only tax collectors come to squeeze levies,
Covetous for bribes from fraudulent dealings,[41]
Gifts[42] or fines for sins we did not commit;[43]
Our only sin—we dare to be alive—
To squeeze the victim's last drop of blood
And in broad daylight rob fruits of hard labor,
The last surviving[44] a drought and flood.

---

40   From Job 9:25.
41   Isa. 33:15.
42   Isa. 1:23.
43   The reverse of a line from Yom Kippur prayers: "For the sin we committed before you."
44   I Chron. 4:43.

The sun has set on all joy[45] in a Jewish home,
Only misery and sorrow are our part,
All joy of Shabbat and Holidays ceased,
And Mitzvah fetes[46] of wedding disappeared,
Instead, funerals keep multiplying...
Misery rules like in a field of graves.

The villagers walk as if dead.
The roads empty, weeds in their cracks
Wagons don't run to bring goods or to take.
For days I am idle cannot earn a wage
Hoping for a miracle, for a little job
A meager one to pay for some feed
For the thin horses, the suffering animals...

The desolation of a graveyard is enduring here.
The best of its young the town spits out,
Like a sick stomach that vomits its food.
Somewhere distant, in the vast world,
Life is glittering, calling and drawing.
Whoever has strong muscles and two hands
Who can conquer the jungle with his own strength
Should come and save his soul that craves life.
With song and good cheer,[47] as if dancing—
The kingdom of Israel is—said to be—reviving

---

45 Isa. 24:11.
46 Reference to the Mitzvah Tantz.
47 From Lekhah Dodi.

Soon in the days that are already coming—
In spite the murderous sons of Ismael our cousins;
A few others travel to distant places
Brazil, Argentina, Chile or Africa
And many other places I could not name.
Only weaklings and old spend here their last days
Waiting for the "liberating death" to take them away...

The coachman turned quiet, took
A last drag of the cigarette in his lips,
Spit to the ground the finished butt
And added hissing—in disdain
That the decaying world is coming to an end
He lashed his horses gently—hinting
That their rest is finally coming.

The village homes look to me like white tombstones on the graves of my youth.
I pray in vain for tears to soften the heavy rock weighing on my numbed heart:
Which was hardened like steel by the mallet of indifference on the anvil of time.
There is only one grave mark that could speak to the mute, dulled heart—
This is father's old home, once a tender blessed nest, still standing there.
Giant waves of old memories engulf my tired, dried, and spent spirit.
I am swept by the waves and descend to the depths of an ancient past.

So good to watch again for but a moment the sights of ancient treasures so dear,
So pleasant it is to dredge up pearls hidden in the mysteries of the depths—
It is so nice for an impoverished man at times to forget his poverty[48]
While remembering his riches that were abundant in days past.

Father's home! Like a baby on his mom's arm with his mouth at her breast
So did it cling lovingly to the Beit Midrash[49] sucking the glow of its holy glory.
Melancholic chants of pleas of repentance or the joyous sounds of studies late night,
And at times the devotees' exhilaration when dancing to celebrate a joy of mitzvah,
Penetrated through the open windows of the house only feet away
Filling its space, absorbing in my heart and melting in my mind blood.
It is paltry and modest from the outside as if imparted by its denizens' spirits.
Flower beds did not grace its small front yard nor a fruiting tree,
A meager young willow with barely a crown did never put down roots,

---

48 Prov. 31:7.
49 Jewish study hall.

Symbolizing the family that came from afar to live in the Polesian lowland—[50]

It stood by the door sad, longing for waters of distant rivulets—

Shy the house stood humble, recoiling modestly from any pretense,

Giving up much of its space for a recess from the street line

In favor of his favorite Beit Midrash . . .

And indoors, the small modest rooms did not dazzle with beauty or boon.

My back exhausted from studying Torah would find rest at night

On a straw bag and a small pad for pillow laid on three old chairs,

Simple wood furniture advanced in years[51] creaked under my bones' weight,

And when litigants[52] stayed late night, my chairs taken up for the trial—

My mother set my bed on an ancient trunk, its paint fading from old age.

Crippled was this crate, one of its steel wheels was lost in earlier years:

But precious to our mother it was, holding remnant treasures of her youth:

---

50 A vast area in the western part of East Europe, stretching through Poland, Ukraine and Belarus.
51 From Gen. 24:1.
52 Rabbi Pearlmutter also acted as an arbitrator.

Scraps of fine silk and worn-out satin decorated with fringes and cross-stitch,
Witnesses of her glowing wedding day full of flowery hopes for the coming days.
But the flowers wilted soon; so did mom very young under her hardships...
Like an inverted hammock was the top of this crate, which doubled as my bed,
I lay sleepless like on a camel's back trying to stay atop without rolling off.

The whitewashed walls were faded, a shade of blue now to their plain white,
Paltiel the plasterer, blind in one eye, expert in mixing colors
And singing *"Dror Yikra"*[53] in *Wulach*[54] tipsy style during the third meal,[55]
Artfully and skillfully painted the walls in early spring year after year.
A straight blue line he drew a smidgen under the roof framed the wall,
And miracle of miracles, bless Palti's one eye, the line was straight time after time.

---

53 "He will proclaim freedom," a piyyut traditionally sung during Shabbat meals.
54 Expressing an elegiac mood.
55 One is obligated to have three meals on Shabbat, one in the morning, one in the afternoon and one in the evening.

A shabby and hoarse wall-clock like a black spot between the east-facing
Windows announced the time to read the daily prayer's Shema.[56]
Lying on its top a remnant of "*Shmurah*,"[57] was waiting from Pesach to Nissan,[58]
Whenever the eye caught its sight, it brought longing to the Pesach nights,
Full of splendor and vivacity, enchanting by their glorious sanctity.

Faces of two old rabbis looked at us from pictures on the white walls,
Bought for pittance from a wandering peddler with a bag on his back...
Their wise eyes expressed love, child's innocence and sadness for the exiled divine,
They radiated like pearls in their humble faces framed by their silvery beards
And inspired faith and trust and infused the heart with a pleasant serenity.
An *Etz Hayim*[59] calendar or "*Mea Shearim*" spread out comfortably between them

---

[56] The centerpiece of the daily morning and evening prayers proclaiming that "The Lord is One."
[57] Though the term "Shmurah" *Matzah* refers to a matzah prepared under strict kosher observance, the reference here is to a piece of the afikoman that was saved from one Passover until the eve of the next as an omen to protect the house.
[58] The seventh month of the Jewish calendar, the month of Pesach.
[59] A Jewish liturgical calendar.

With pictures showing the Western Wall the survivor of the wicked Titus's fire,
With two date trees standing ready like sentries on each of its sides;
And Rachel's Tomb with its green dome standing by the red tent[60]
Both reminding our rabbi's lovely and enchanting hymn of "*Va'Ani*."[61]
"Jerusalem the holy city shall be built and well-founded speedily in our days, Amen"[62]
These letters made the eyes light up[63] hinting of something sacred and so desired
Immersed in dreams and concealed secrets waiting and waiting for their resolution . . . .

---

60 It is not clear what is the red tent that is mentioned here.
61 "As for me" in Hebrew; from a liturgic poem: "As for me, nearness to God is good" (Ps. 73:28).
62 One of the ten remembrances a Jew must recite during the morning prayer.
63 Ps. 19:9.

The Old Doc[64]

The terrain is plagued.
Shattered in battle
By bolts of rain
From Fall, its rival.

Lying in pain[65]
Our Mother Earth
Anguished, hurt,
Barely a breath in her.

Every field barren,
Valleys decaying,
Every disease and wound[66]
Stuck to her flesh.

Oozing mucus and sludge
Deep is her mud,
All are tired of
Inhaling her air.

Heavens pitied her
Mourned her surrender
Grief engulfed the Earth
And all it holds.[67]

---

64 From the collection of Avrom Bendavid-Val.
65 From Isa. 50:11.
66 From Jer. 6:7.
67 From Ps. 24:1.

Then came the savior,
Riding on a cloud crown
Dressed in pure white—
The old doc,

Swabbed everyone's tears,
Cheered people up:
His forceps wrung
Out all painful hurts—

Refreshed every morning[68]
From heavens above
He brought down
Downy white snow,

Dressed her with
Gauze all around
Administered sleeping drugs
To drowse her till spring.

Then will Mother
Earth reawaken to life,
Fresh, blooming,
Healthy and sound.

---

68   Lam. 3:23.

Beneath the Crescent Moon[69]

The village slumbers
Amid the woods,
I am still awake
Beneath the crescent moon.

The brook too
Never reposes—
Crescent and I
On its ripples we float.

My raft
Carries me;
A silvery crescent
Is following me,

Somewhat curved
No extremities;
But it is as agile
As a fish in the stream.

My oars splash
Tif! Tif! Tif!
The silent crescent
Remains still.

---

69 From the collection of Avrom Bendavid-Val.

I inhale deeply
Midnight's essence,
Velvety dew,
Silvery air

Overwhelmed by scent
Of reed and hay—
My whole body
Joyfully unwinds.

But the crescent, naught
Like a clueless fool,
Pale, drained of blood,
Soundless like a rock—

Spring Has Run Away...[70]

Hustle-bustle in the streets—
The town fair is humming.
In the tumult,
Are engulfed
Modest steps of spring.

No one suspects that spring
Is close to the town, not too far.
Deaf, blind,
People are busy,
Running, fussing—loud cries.

Smoothly pressed and new, the sky
Holiday-like, the sunshine
Here in town,
A chaos reigns
An insolent wild dance

Impatiently, cars push forward,
Like frogs, here, there,
Croaking, whistling
Leaving behind
a sharp smell of gas.

---

70 Originally published in *Mezryczer Trybune*, issue 12 (March 21, 1930), 3. My thanks to Ellen Cassedy for her assistance in translating from Yiddish.

Horse drawn wagons
Creep forward brazen:
A crack of a whip:
—Make way
For the hairy-pig freight!

In the wagon we see a hog,
Tied fast to the cart
—I want freedom!—"
He bellows
In sharp piggish gripe.

A mix of voices, languages,
A jumble of people and cows;
Booths, shops,
Tables, wagons—
Who is thinking of spring now?—

In the clamor
Every higher thought
is drowned
Swindling Trading—
That's all anyone wants.

No regard to the spring;
No apt preparations made
To welcome
With due respect
Such an esteemed guest.

So the guest, humiliated, tarries outside
Disappointed
And soon makes a decision
Turns around—
And hurries away

Now the sky is wrapped
In dark mourning-clothes
And winter
Takes control
Spreading itself upon the earth once more

*

The wind whistles. A deep bass voice calls:
Look, you blind people . . . ! Listen, you deaf!
Spring has run away from you
Well, you don't deserve it yet. . . .

Międzyrzecz, 1930

צבי קרול

למיכ"ר

בשנת המאה לתולדתו.

בְּמִסְתָּרֵי-אָהֳלִי בְּאֵין רוֹאֶה,
בַּצּוֹרֵף חַזְּךְ לַיְלָה, לַיְלָה אֲחַזֶּה יִגוֹנִי
אֲשֶׁר רִמְּסוּהוּ-יַצָּב, סַלְעֵי-נְּעוּרִים
וְחֵן-עֶרֶב לִי תּוּעֲמוּ כִּתְפָחִים וְנִיחוֹחִים...

עֵצוּר בְּאַבֵּי-חֵידַת מִתְגַּעַשׁ בְּפִתְחֵי-מוֹ
אֶל דּוּר-שֶׁעֲרִי אֶדְרֹד עֵינֵיי-רוּךְ
אֶזְכְּרָה לִינוּן עוֹלָם חוֹבֵר לִי מִשָּׁם
וּלְכָבִי בִּי יִגְוַע מַצְרִית אֲחֶרֶת...

רְנָעוֹת יָדַי לְגַל פְּרָח נָבֵל שֶׁכְּפַר
וְנַפְשִׁי חָכְכָה לֶאֱנָשִׁים חֲתוּלִים
סֵבֶל הָאוֹמוּת אֶצְרַף שָׁם — חָנֶה
וְאֵרָאֶה דְפֻקָּתָה עַל סִבְרִי נוֹסַפְתָה...

בְּמִסְתָּרֵי-אָהֳלִי בְּאֵין רוֹאֶה,
בַּצּוֹרֵף חַזְּךְ לַיְלָה, לַיְלָה אֲחַזֶּה יִגוֹנִי
אֲשֶׁר רִמְּסוּהוּ-יַצָּב, סַלְעֵי-נְּעוּרִים
וְחֵן-עֶרֶב לִי תּוּעֲמוּ כִּתְפָחִים וְנִיחוֹחִים...

בְּמִסְתָּרֵי-אָהֳלִי בְּאֵין רוֹאֶה,
בַּצּוֹרֵף חַזְּךְ לַיְלָה, לַיְלָה אֲחַזֶּה יִגוֹנִי
אֲשֶׁר רִמְּסוּהוּ-יַצָּב, סַלְעֵי-נְּעוּרִים
וְחֵן-עֶרֶב לִי תּוּעֲמוּ כִּתְפָחִים וְנִיחוֹחִים...

אַךְ אֲנִי אָאִיר מוּזָר — וְהִיא מֵצִין חַבְרָכַת
וְחַיִּים לֹא אֲסַלֵּל — וְחָם מִשְׂחָק בְּמוֹת,
לְלִבִּי לֹא יָגַע בְּגָדֵי-צִבְרִי-נוֹסַף-רָע
וְשַׂפְתַּי לֹא יִקְּאוּ נִיבֵי גְדִי וְקָפָּץ...

י. בידר

על בלימה

יוֹרֵד שֶׁפַע לְבַן מְסַנְוֵר עַל אֳגַן שָׂדוֹת.
אֵבֶר שְׁבוּלִי לְחָרִים בְּסַפְלוֹת וּבְמַדְרוֹנוֹת...
חֲמוֹקֵי שְׁעוּעִים נָאִים, גּוֹאֲנִים בְּגֶנֶם קוֹלֵס,
וְכַּצִי שָׁטוּ גְּלִים מְסַתּוֹבְבִים בְּמָרוֹלָם.

אֵיפֹה חַסְפָּסִיַּת? — נָפַלְנוּ בְּסַם-מַחֲבוֹר,
עוֹבְרֵי-אָרְחָה נוֹעָנִים, וְרַדְמוּ אָחֲרוּ אִבֵד:
בְּחֵרוּם שְׁאָטוּ סִבְכֵּנוּ, שֶׁפַע אֹרַז עוֹלָם...
פְרָחֵי שַׁלֵּנוּ וְחוֹרֵשׁוֹ שָׂרִים לְגַן מִצְרַם.

עוֹלָם כֻּלּוֹ הַפַּסְף... עָווּב בְּמָאֲמִנוּ,
לֹא יֶרְגִּישׁ בְּרִיחְמוֹתָל, לֹא יִתְגַּע אֵת אֲלָּתוֹ...
וְאֵין מִי גַם יוֹדֵעַ לוֹ, וְאֵין מִי חַדִּיל דָּפְקָה?
וִי שֶׁל עוֹלָם תְּלוּשָׁם, תַּלְוּי בְּנֶגֶם עַל בְּלִימָה!...

א. א. קבק

הקרבן

ספר שלישי מתוך הטרילוגיה "שלמה מיכבי"

(המשך)

"כלום לא הרגשת שהאשם די לוּפוֹ גם הוא מצא בך אדם קרוב להתיישבות הנוצרית? הוא ראה בך אדם ואולי גם קדוש שהולך בעקבות תלמיכו, וכסאן מקור כל רעש ואפלי ואהבתו אליך..."

"ואאמור די לופו, אינני כלל נוצרי, ר"ל זה מכבר כפר בתורות הסתוולדייריומים; בזמנו יש איזו ערבוביה מתהוונות הדתיות של הברות המיניים שעבורו בין הנוצרים. בחיבור בנגד אשכנז זו...
"כן ואמרות די לוסף הוא כזה בדוחי. ואף-על-פי-כן לא נעקרה עדיני סלבי חורתם של נוירי מנגד תירווניםים בלם. ואף אתה כן. אם בך יותת ענייו תלמוים של הנוצרים האלה, הכיצים עליך חיומרים לא מסיבה שבאים בתור עונש מן השמים, אלא מפני שם נוסלים. מפני שבנמה משהו בתוך נפשם ואת נפש אחרים. אתה אוהב להיות קרבן?"

— קרבן! — הוסיף טלבי להתיוכח עם הסוף שבלבי שאתה' עשה ולא רעה לחשבתך. — ומה בכך? כלום אבותינו שנתנו על קירשיהשם. נפשות אהיו מלבינם. נחת ישבנה בונית. ואלסי אחינו הנגריים במסתרי האינקויזיציה. כלום כל אלה סבלו ומתו וסובלים וסימת בתור נוצרים? נוצרים יצאה האם זה?"
"ואת-על-פי-כן...," ואף-על-פי-כן..." התעצצה חפל שבלב — כל אותם הוררים של קרוש-השם הצער חיים וסמם לכוחות, רמתם בא מתוך אנם ובפיה. הוא הוא צרה שנגרים עליהם לפנם השטים והצדיקו עליהם את נוחני וצחתל את נוצלים לעצם במשת כל ימי. מלחשתונו על נוירויברה. לעצלה זו של הנשמה מן הצרות היא... אתה הצמן בצער חיבוריים שנתקסים. מסוברים לומסטים ואתה כפעם. משאות מאת מהן היי הרעה ורועד דחם... לא בנוירה מן השטים היו לך, שמיינו אורש לסקלף באהבה."

The Land of Israel

On the Edge[1]

A blast of white blinding light descends over the fields,
The trail to the mountains was lost uphill and downhill . . .

Herds of goats[2] appeared with their young bleating,
And the sons of Satan all spun in their dance.

Where are the Heavens?—The Throne of Glory disappeared.
Wayfarers are lost, and many are gone, vanished:

Enmeshed in the devil's ban, blinded by the boundless whiteness:
Devils toss snow flowers over their graves . . .

The entire world is forsaken, frozen and neglected,
Not sensing its isolation, not demanding satisfaction for its humiliation.

No one would feel sorry for it. Whose eye would shed a tear?
Alas, for an entire world detached, and only by miracle hanging off the edge! . . .

---

1 Courtesy of the United States Holocaust Memorial Museum—The Israel Beider collection and the collection of Avrom Bendavid-Val. Previously published in *Ha-Olam*, issue 9 (March 1, 1929), 177.
2 In the context of the "goat to Azazel," Lev. 16:7–9.

Who Is the Hebrew![3]

On primeval hilltops swathed in secrets
A sign on a flag is emblazoned with fire:
Who is the Hebrew who had his fill of the nomadic tent
And would silently weep over his eternal exile,
He should come to build!
Whose ears are burning with fiery talk
Born in a foreign land during the nation's wandering
Singing the song of the nation's prophets
Lend a hand to bring the dream about.

---

[3] Courtesy of the United States Holocaust Memorial Museum—The Israel Beider collection and the collection of Avrom Bendavid-Val. A note on the manuscript states that this poem was published in Tkhiyatenu, but the publication's issue number and date could not be confirmed.

Excursion in the Homeland[4]

Haifa, a perfectly beautiful[5] big city.
My flat[6]—a shack—in Hadar Ha-Carmel.[7]
Dear to me is my picturesque, pure city,
Its golden sun descending into the sea.

Dear to me are her myriad sons,
Guarding, creating, working, building.
At the port, in the shop, by hand or on shoulder
And Hebrew songs streaming from their lips.

On my days off, when my work is done
I yearn for the land and its splendor—
See all that enchanted me in exile
Whose radiance captivated my childhood from afar.

I leave my shack, and the heights of my Carmel,
Walking stick in hand, pack on my back,
I bid good-bye to Haifa and its coast
Her beautiful vistas and shining radiance

---

[4] From the collection of Avrom Bendavid-Val.
[5] From Lam. 2:15.
[6] Beider made unsuccessful attempts to immigrate to Israel but never made it there.
[7] The first Jewish neighborhood in Haifa, halfway up Mt. Carmel on the slope facing the Haifa Bay.

Hiking through valleys and mountains,
By the sides of velvet smooth roads.
I walk in the land and inhale its air
Lips singing and heart full of joy.

My eyes would soak up glorious old sites,
Sanctity of ancient times,—virtuous scholars,
True prophets and heroes of wars
Whose blood soaked every patch of her ground.

I would cling to every valley, gorge, and mount,
Every creek a friend and every hill beloved,
From a fragrant orchard to a pile of rocks—
All wrapped in beauty and mystical aura.

I would carry greetings to every city and *Moshava*,[8]
From the young, vibrant, fair Tel Aviv
Eternally joyful, humming, socializing
To the holy city of Shalem[9] soon to be rebuilt.

I would bless Tiberias too, while not as vast—
Kineret is her crystal sea and the sky her blue canopy.
All is glorious beauty and splendor in the Land of Israel
And the jewel in her crown—the Valley of Jezreel.

---

8   A Jewish agricultural settlement where all land and property are privately owned.
9   Jerusalem, Gen.14:18.

Scenic are its fields and plentiful its herds,
How pleasing are its tents,[10] pioneers and farmers,
All healthy, joyful, cheerfully working,
Its children blossoming like garden flowers.

Thus I will merrily wander in this land of wonders
Where the land is blessed and the skies hallowed
With joyful feelings my song will echo,
When returning full of impressions to my city shack.

---

10 Reference to Num. 24:5.

Lamentations[11]

Alas my heart laments anew
In a mournful tune and silent rage—
Alas: Villains raided my refuge,
Defiled the Third Temple's[12] base.

The *Shekhina* weeps for the Western Wall
Beating hawk's wings—from every direction:
Descending to capture the treasure of the beautiful land[13]
Strength is gone[14] all the ends of days passed.[15]

Like a dismembered body in a lion's paw
Our fathers' land trembles in *Albion's*[16] hand;
The Arab is tearing out a living organ
And the crescent moon[17] hangs over Mount Zion.

---

11 Courtesy of the United States Holocaust Memorial Museum—The Israel Beider collection. This poem is written in Hebrew but was published in a Yiddish paper. The clip does not include its attribution. Printed together with the essay "Today is *Tisha'a be-Av*." From the essay's context it can be assumed that it is referring to the 1936–39 Arab uprising and its consequences.
12 The new Land of Israel is often referred to as the Third Temple even though no such temple was ever built.
13 ארץ הצבי, Dan. 11:41.
14 From Deut. 32:36.
15 A Talmudic expression.
16 An alternative name to Great Britain who was controlling Palestine at the time.
17 Reference to the symbol of Islam.

The ruin of the people is great[18] the pain is immense
Worse is this destruction than in the preceding two,
Because her sons forgot how to fight for their homeland
Gone are the *Bar Kokhbas*, the *Gideons*[19] are no more.

---

18 From Lam. 2:11.
19 Obviously Beider refers to the followers of Gideon the Judge, Judg. 8:22–32, rather than to the evangelical association Gideons International.

Der Pastukh. Image of the printed poem "Der Pastukh – the Shepherd" and the essay "The Modest One." From *Podliasher Tsaytung* [Podliash Journal], Issue 15–16 (April 24, 1937), 2. Courtesy of the United States Holocaust Memorial Museum—The Israel Beider collection.

"Der Pastukh"—The Shepherd[20]

In memory of Avraham Gelman Z"L

There was a shepherd, a poor shepherd,
The days burned him, the nights froze him,
He fed himself mostly on herbs from the field
While lovingly leading the weakling sheep.

The shepherd was a lonely stranger,
Ancient woods concealed his home
There he would clasp his flute to his breast
To the proud high mountain whence fresh waters sprang...

There he sat, the solitary shepherd,
Happy with the sheep as they grazed.
In the glow of the dawn, the evening's crimson
Pouring himself out with the sound of the flute...

There was a shepherd, a poor shepherd—
Who knew, or knew of him?
And suddenly his flute went silent, disappeared,
His heart ceased to beat in his breast.

Only the sheep remember his love, his devotion
And miss his calm step.
In the glow of the dawn, the crimson of evening
Miss his sad, gentle song.

---

20 Courtesy of the United States Holocaust Memorial Museum—The Israel Beider collection. Previously published in the *Podliasher Tsaytung* [Podliash journal], issue 15–16 (April 24, 1937), 2. Translated from Yiddish by Andrew Cassel. A headline at the top of the page indicates that it was a memorial tribute to Avraham Gelman, 5647–5697 (i.e., 1887–1937).

Father's Home. Image of the handwritten first page of the poem "Father's Home." Courtesy of the United States Holocaust Memorial Museum—The Israel Beider collection.

Family

Father's Home[1]

... Glorious rays of supreme holiness and spiritual splendor
radiated in the air
The heavy and thick books, which filled and crammed the
plain cabinet,
Piled on top of it, and even cluttered the long table,
in the study room.
Research, Kabbalah, Aggadah,[2] Halacha[3] merged here in a
wondrous fusion;
One did not encroach on the other across the boundaries of
naïve, and pure faith;
All were overlain by the holy Torah and illuminated by its
bright rays.
The Talmud and its "squires" the Maimonides,[4]
"Ha-Turim,"[5] and the four "Shulchan Aruch"[6]

---

1 Courtesy of the United States Holocaust Memorial Museum—The Israel Beider collection and the collection of Avrom Bendavid-Val.
2 A type of rabbinic literature.
3 Jewish Law.
4 Referring to Mishneh Torah, authored by Moshe ben Maimon, commonly known as Maimonides, and referred here by the acronym Rambam (רמב״ם).
5 Ba'al Ha-Tourim or Rabbi Ya'akov ben Asher, an influential rabbinic authority, author of Arba'ah Turim [Four columns], among the most important halachic books of the time.
6 A widely accepted compilation of Jewish laws.

And questions and answers, the first and the last,[7]
—a wonderful legion of the Torah,
Clinging so lovingly to the "Akedah,"[8] "Ikkarim,"[9]
"Moreh ha-Nevuchim,"[10] and the "Kuzari,"[11]
And Tikkunei Zohar[12] mated with "Bina La'Itim"[13]
and "Parashat Derachim."[14]
Generations and epochs of thousands of years formed
here one unit.
Aren't all streams flow to the sea,[15] this is the deep sea
of the Torah;
And all the footpaths lead to the main road—
The King of the World . . .
No one would run over the other: here young and
old live together on a level field,
The four hundred years old Tur, one of the first
printings of *Venedik*[16]
In its thick covers of leather over wood plates and its thick pages

---

7   Reference to the earlier and later interpretations of the Torah laws.
8   Reference to the Binding of Isaac.
9   *Sefer Ha-Ikkarim* [Book of principles]: an exposition of the principles of Judaism.
10 Guide for the perplexed a work of theology by Maimonides.
11 *The Kuzari* was written by Judah Halevi (Spain, 1075–1141). It describes how the king of the Khazars (an Asian tribe) converted along with his entire tribe to Judaism after finding it to be the true religion.
12 A major kabbalistic text.
13 A work by Rabbi Azarya Figo (1579–1647), which is still popular today, particularly amongst *Mizrahi* (Oriental) Jews, entitled Binah La'Ittim, which contains seventy-five sermons for Shabbat and holidays.
14 A work by Judah Rosanes (1657–1727) holding twenty-six homiletic treatises on various subjects.
15 Eccl. 1:7.
16 Venice in Yiddish. The first printing of the Tur was made in Piove di Sacco about 15 miles from Venice.

Green from age and black in their margins from rubbing by the
fingers of generations,
As if each generation tried to leave its lasting mark
a memorial for the future—
Stood here in tandem with "Divrei Malkiel"[17]
—which only now saw the light of the day—
displaying its new thick binding with its shiny gold trimmings.

Father took short and long walks in the "Pardes"[18]
of the holy Torah
And found refuge for his weary soul in its shade,
and satiated its hunger with its fruit
And quenched his thirst in its well-springs of wisdom burbling
among its mountains of parchments.
His never-ending chanting vibrated between
the home's walls day and night.
The melody of mute books sweetened his meager and
bitter portion.
Until sleep shut his eyes like the lullaby of a good mother
to her child,
Erasing the memory of the tortures he endured
At the hands of soldiers who caught him for service to the
Russian kingdom.
This book became the source of his life, destination of his being,
His playmate, shelter from his plights, refuge,
citadel at a time of trouble.

17　Talmudic commentary by Malkiel Tzvi Tenenboim, Rabbi of Lomzha (1847–1910).
18　Literally an orchard. But in this context, a reference to the mysteries of the Kabbalah.

At the dawn of summer mornings, quenched by dew and
saturated with scents of fresh hay,
And pine forests, greening like bouquets at the margins of
golden wheat fields;
When the face of the rising sun turned bright, coating the walls
with sheets of red;
Before the shepherd's blowing horn broke the sweet silence
To wake up the cows, who regurgitated in their serene sleep;
Even before elder Jews with talith bags under their arms
Imprinted with their heavy shoes on the street's sands the signs
of a new day—
Father was already sitting by the hallowed table laden
with the heavy books.
He was sailing into the vast seas, crossed their titanic
and deep waters,
Dipped his soul in their pure, refreshing and cleansing waves.
Precious glow in his eyes from the abundant bliss, and his
meager and gloomy face,
Radiated in a supreme luminosity, expressing eternal joy.
Every corner was filled then by the sweet tunes gurgling from
his mouth
A magical melody saturated with yearning to discover the
secrets within
The parchments, the primeval letters, the acronyms and the
miniscule vocalizations,[19]
And as I was lying in the adjacent room on the buckling and
rocking crate,
The melody vibrated my ear drums and infused
its sweetness into my sleep.

---

19 *Nikud*, נִקּוּד, the Hebrew way to mark vowels in text.

Or that too would happen—that father, overjoyed by the sight
of the birth of a new day,
In the midst of an all-encompassing wonderful nature, as the
sun would emerge above the treetops;
As the universe would wake up in its multitudes of colors and
its myriads of images
And inspiring sounds that coalesce into a wonderful supreme
harmony;
While young lives, fresh and powerful gush energetically
From each lump of earth, every shrub and grass, from buzzing
and chirping sounds
By a choir of thousands of creatures singing for the new queen,
Who marches fearlessly under a giant blueish canopy—
He would rise off his chair, close his book slowly with
a loving kiss
And in measured and balanced steps, like one who walks along
a known paved road,
He would stroll from one wall to the other—back and forth—
And in a rhythm that emanates from the bottom of his soul he
would sing in an ultimate devotion:
I shall thank the Lord, Searcher of the Heart[20]
When the morning stars sang together...[21]
And his emotion would overflow, and his voice would express
yearning
For salvation from the darkness engulfing his murky
bodily matter,

---

20 This and the next verse are part of a song of dawn; an introductory prayer upon rising.
21 Job 38:7.

Which prevents his soul from beholding the divine glory of the real world:
Resplendent, beautiful, radiance of the world,[22]
My soul is sick for your amore ...
For so much has this yearning been,
To see your strength, in its beauty ...
Rouse, please, your mercy
Have pity, please, and do not conceal yourself.
And like a son nestling up against his father, nags him and pleads,
Asking to take him along to show him the wonders of the capital city—
That's how father speaks to God Most High[23] and pours his feelings:
Ho, Ho, please have pity merciful father
Have pity, please, and do not conceal yourself.
And I had a vision in my sleep: the "Lower *Gan Eden*" is around me,
A palace of gold, flooded by the light of the seven days,[24] turned into our home;
Amid wonderful boulevards and trees, no eye of flesh has ever seen such
Old righteous are strolling there along with smiling rabbis
Enjoying the glory of the holy divine and their talking is teeming with melodies ....

---

22 This and the next five verses are from "Yedid Nefesh" [Beloved of the soul], a Jewish hymn, usually sung on Shabbat.
23 Gen. 14:18.
24 Isa. 30:26.

Work[25]

I was very tired and laid down on the couch to rest. I
Thought to get refreshed by a little nap. But that was not
What my four-year-old toddler had on his mind. He saw
That I was lying on the couch, quickly jumped on me. Sat
By me, hugged my neck with his tender arms, looked straight
Into my eyes and started talking:
-Please don't sleep, dad. Is it night now?
-I am tired though, my lovely son. Let me nap
A bit—I begged him.
But my plea was for naught.
-What is tired?—The toddler wondered.
-It means that I am drained, and I need to rest.
-And why is that you are drained? - He asked
Out of curiosity.
I did not want to answer, but I was worried
That he will feel offended by my silence,
So I replied briefly:
-Because I worked.
My toddler turned quiet. I thought his questions came to
An end. My eyelids turned heavy and almost
closed on their own.
I nearly started dozing off.
But I was wrong. Not even a few minutes and here was

---

25 Courtesy of the United States Holocaust Memorial Museum—The Israel Beider collection. A slightly different version is included in the Avrom Bendavid-Val collection. This translation follows the version held by the USHMM.

A voice ringing out:[26]

-And who is ordering you to work?—

I opened my eyes reluctantly and answered in a feeble voice:

-All the people work—and closed my eyes again.

-But why? Who orders them to do so?—I hear

My son's voice and once again my eyes are forced to open.

I looked

At my son's face as he was sitting by me and it express a big

Incredulity and an expectation for an answer, as if it is truly necessary for him

To get an answer to his question. And one more thing

I realized: He does not worry at all that I will get mad at him,

For bothering me with his questions and disturbing my rest.

He certainly recognizes his power, which is reinforced by his beautiful

Eyes, his tousled curls and pink lips!

-That's the way of the world my son—I said—everyone

Needs to work, and after work—take a rest.

-And the children?—the little one kept asking and caressed

My forehead gently with his fingers.

I saw that there is no end to the questions

And they keep coming and coming like "a fountain that gathers force,"[27]

And I say to myself: let me try for once not to answer

---

26 From Isa. 40:3.
27 A Talmudic expression, e.g., Pirkei Avot 2.

My son. Maybe he will leave me alone.
But he thought otherwise:
When he saw that I am not answering at once he raised his voice
Straight into my ear: "Dad! Dad!" I was alarmed.
-What's wrong son? I asked, startled.
-Tell me—he lowered his voice a bit—And the children?
Why don't they work?
They are little—I answered—when they grow up, they will work too.
-And me?—The toddler kept asking after half
A moment of silence—and I what will I do?
What kind of work?
-When you grow up you will choose a job for yourself, whichever you wish.
-Tell me dad, what is a good thing to be? Which
Work is better?
Any work is good for a man when he is healthy.
But my son did not find satisfaction with this answer.
-But please tell me what should I be?
He called out in a slight protest.
Whatever you want—I said and got off the couch
Realizing that I will not be able to nap—teacher, doctor . . .
-I don't want to be a teacher. A teacher punishes
The mischievous children . . .
I put on my coat, took my walking cane and
walked to the door.
My son ran after me:
Just a moment dad! Is it true that it is not good
Being a teacher? It is better to make oranges.

Yes, yes, son—true I answered just to fulfill
My obligation.[28]
-Where do oranges grow? Mom said that in
The land of Israel.
-Yes, yes, son. They grow on trees in the land of Israel.
-I know. I ate an orange when I was ill.
It tastes good. That's when mom told me ...
-When you grow up, son, you will go to the land of Israel
And work in an orange grove.
-That will be very nice, the toddler commented
And his eyes glow with joy. When will I travel there?
-When you grow up—my sweet. I kissed him on his cheek
and left.
Behind the door I heard him asking:
-And when will I grow up? ...

---

28   A Talmudic expression, e.g., Shulkhan Arukh, Orakh Khayim, 690.

Sarah is Departing[29]

I still remember. And whenever I recall
The chilling scene appears before my eyes
It shook me to the depths of my soul
And tears flow from my eyes.

Full of light red like blood
The sun was sinking into the sea
Knowing that sunset is nigh.
My soul was churning.

In steady degrees the sun
Kept descending
When it grazed treetops
Sorrow filled my heart

Pulsing veins in my core
Waking to agony in my soul
My blood boiling like fire
Looming over my life like a cloud.

The wagon stood by all ready
Sacks stacked high in bundles
A piercing sound echoed in my heart
You are leaving to a faraway land

Women and children began to cry
The ebbing day reminds me it's time
The moment is at hand
Time for her departure has come . . . .

---

29 From the collection of Avrom Bendavid-Val.

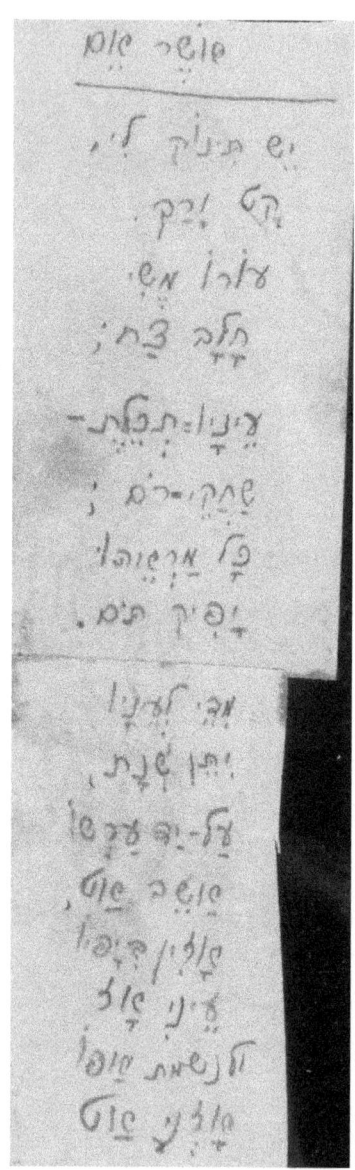

Motherly Bliss. Image of the handwritten original of the poem "Motherly Bliss." Courtesy of the United States Holocaust Memorial Museum—The Israel Beider collection.

Motherly Bliss[30]

I have an infant,	All his fussing	Wealth and fortune
Small and new,	Splendid magic,	Why do I need them?
Silk-like skin	His dream's smile	My son's eyes,
Milky white;	Wrapped in secret,	Sparkling sapphires,
His eyes are blue—	His tiny lips	His crown of hair
Like the sky above,	Slowly quiver,	Pure gold
His entire look	His lush cheeks—	Why should I dread
Bright and pure.	Crimson bright—	Poverty or want—

When his eyes	My eyes see all.
close to sleep,	My heart hums
By his crib	Babbling with joy
I silently sit,	Like a pure brook.
Feast on his beauty	Burden of woes,
With my eyes,	Bitter fate,
And quietly absorb	Daily worries—
His gentle gurgles.	Are all gone

---

30 Courtesy of the United States Holocaust Memorial Museum—The Israel Beider collection, and the collection of Avrom Bendavid-Val. The version displayed by the USHMM includes only two stanzas; the remaining stanzas are from the Avrom Bendavid-Val collection. The format here matches the version in the Bendavid-Val collection.

The Photograph[31]

You are near my heart like a pretty amulet
It is your image preserved on a photograph
Cold and shiny like an icicle.

On rainy nights in a gloomy world
When terrifying winds rage and howl,
Uprooting trees in combative roars—

I would look at it and silently intone as in a prayer
The inscription on the reverse
"Remember me!" "Forever remember me!"

Then suns that set in my heart will rise,
A forgotten song will be remembered
Past springs will live again with joyful cheers.

---

31 From the collection of Avrom Bendavid-Val.

To Ya'akov[32]

In my dreams at night, I envision us close again
Vast lands and gushing depths of seas[33] vanished.
Great distances shrunk and walls and horizons
No longer stand between two loving brothers.

My highest wishes fulfilled—we breath one air
Like oceans' strength and seas' breaking waves
Our feelings spawn holy fire, spirits and flames
Gurgling gushing from hearts—like springs.

Brother in brother's arms we unite and cling.
And the air absorbs the fete of our pouring love
That bursts like a gale into a wreath of kisses.
From above the joyful stars watch and quietly listen . . .

"I saw the ocean's face
Boiling humming, breaking waves—
    So is my heart humming and boiling
        My lips at your lips kissing when you're coming! . . ."

"As one giant wave chasing the other
Like the impulse of a formidable gale
    So does my emotion topping the next
        When I press thee to my chest" . . .

---

32   From the collection of Avrom Bendavid-Val.
33   From Ps. 68:23.

"As the depths of the great deep[34] shake,
Like an ocean overflowing the land
>> So does my heart tremble and flutter
>> When the mixture of its emotions erupts"....

"Like bubbles skipping over waves
Like sunlight breaking into myriad sparks
>> So does my heart overflow with light
>> Light of flames of a fire—fiery-love..."

This did my lips whisper in my dream
The brotherhood when we meet—
These are my dreams in my nightly sleep
Dream, Ha. Reunion in my dream...

---

34 Gen. 7:11.

You are Bar Mitzvah . . . . Image of the card written by Yisrael Beider to his nephew Moshe, the son of his brother Rabbi Ya'akov Pearlmutter. From the collection of Avrom Bendavid-Val.

You are Bar Mitzvah...[35]

To Moshe the son of my brother Rabbi Ya'akov Pearlmutter,[36] *Mazal Tov* for the *Bar Mitzvah*-day.

a

Wear tall the symbol![37]
Joyfully on your head
Shrouded by the Shekhinah—
You are Bar Mitzvah today!

b

A symbol for you
Banner of love
To your wandering people—
Old Man Israel...

c

Should the burden be heavy
And the road demanding—
All your laboring
God will be blessing!

---

35 From the collection of Avrom Bendavid-Val.
36 This poem was sent in May 1939 by its author, Yisrael Beider, to Marvin (Moshe) Pearlmutter, his nephew in Baltimore, on the occasion of his Bar Mitzvah.
37 The word used by Sefaria.org to describe the head piece of the phylacteries (טטפת Deut. 6:8).

d

The baggage more precious
Than pearls and gold;
Life eternal for your
Nation it holds...

e

Eternal life
No limits no end—
Remember always:
You are Bar Mitzvah today!

f

This is the blessing
From me in this tribute:
Blossom and thrive
Be a source of pride

g

Celebrated by our nation
Adored by your parents
Your name will endure
From generation to generation

With lots of love – your uncle Yisrael

When the Eighth Candle Dies Out. Image of the handwritten original of the poem "When the Eighth Candle Dies Out." Courtesy of the United States Holocaust Memorial Museum—The Israel Beider collection.

Oppression

When the Eighth Candle Dies Out[1]

A candle[2] was bright and soon died out
The oil ran out, the wick burned out,
And the *menorah* was stored out of sight
No more glee, and no more light

There was a miracle—and it is gone
Where is the time of wonders divine?
Light prevailed, but only for a short while,
And once again dark's dominion reigns . . . .

Oh, who would grant me a menorah
With a lit candle of eternal flame,
To scare away shadows and bitter times
And illuminate forever my dark nights!

---

1 Courtesy of the United States Holocaust Memorial Museum—The Israel Beider collection. This poem was previously published in *Ha-Kokhav* [The star] on 8 Tevet 5684 (December 16, 1923). Ha-Kokhav was a youth bi-weekly paper which provided an open platform for young aspiring writers and poets to publish their works; it was published by Aron Luboszycki between 1923–1928.
2 The eighth candle is the last Hanukkah candle, lit on the eighth day of the holiday.

The Orphan[3]

Night after night at midnight
Orphan baby's sleep is disturbed:[4]
Suddenly he wakes out of his
Sweet sleep—startled.
He looks around, searches–
Mother's bed is empty ...
Where is she that late at night?
He went to sleep at her bosom,
Cuddled gently in her arms
She kissed him lovingly,
Pressing him to her snugly
Her heart almost touching his heart!?
Poor child moaned bitterly
Little orphan sobbed dreadfully:
His eyes so innocent
Expressing surprise and fright.

---

3   From the collection of Avrom Bendavid-Val. Previously published in *Ha-Kokhav*, Iyar 7688 (May 1928).
4   From Esther 6:1.

Orphaned baby moaned again–
Raising his voice wailing,
Through the night baby wept
Until dawn broke the dark.
All through the night he cried bitterly:
"Mother, Mother, Mother!"
His copious tears streamed
Drowning his crib under the flood.
He fell asleep as dawn of another
Hopeless day—was on the horizon
A tear drying on his cheek
From sobbing in his sleep.

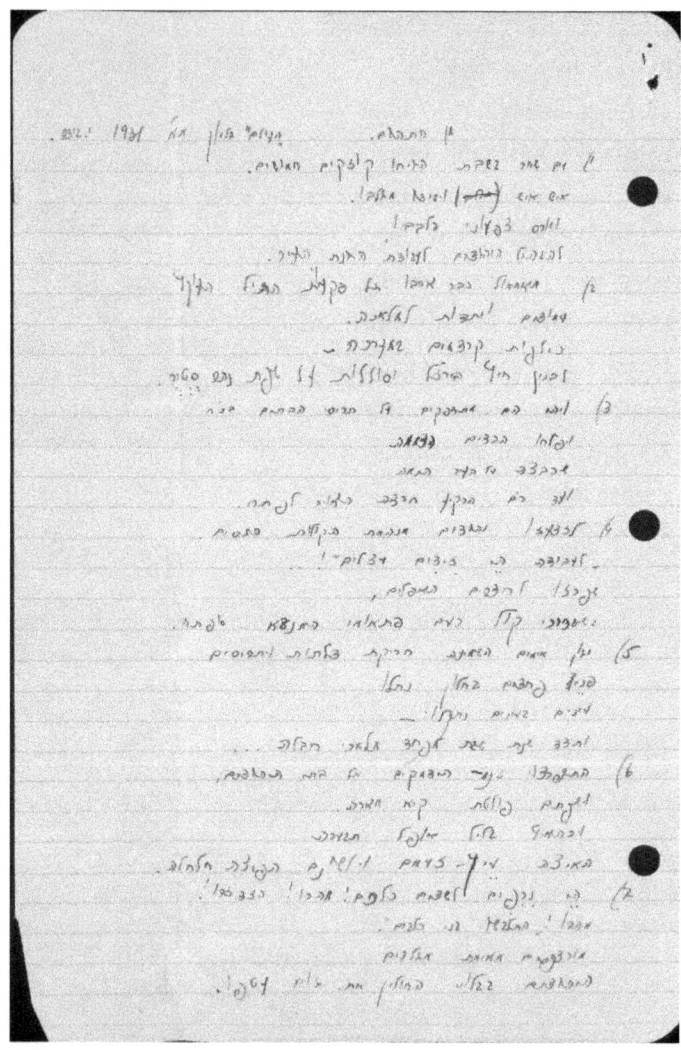

From the Abyss. Image of the handwritten first page of the poem "From the Abyss." Courtesy of the United States Holocaust Memorial Museum—The Israel Beider collection and the Avrom Bendavid-Val collection.

From the Abyss[5]

At dawn on Shabbat armed Cossacks appeared,
> Each one with a crop in hand
> And serpent's venom in his heart,
To roundup Jews for labor for the "city's defense."

Lurking since yesterday were: piles of barbed wires,
> Poles, stakes and tools for the workers,
> Pikes[6] and axes all ready for battle—
To build iron walls and levies on the River Styr's[7] banks.

As they banged violently on window shutters—
> Echoes pierced the quiet,
> Still suspending over the sleeping city,
A fear of opening doors hung in the air and rose to the heavens.

The Jews were shaken by growls of coarse voices:
> "Up to work you lazy *Zhyds*"....[8]
> The sounds reverberated into dark rooms
Like sudden thunderclaps announcing the storm.

---

5   Courtesy of the United States Holocaust Memorial Museum—The Israel Beider collection and the Avrom Bendavid-Val collection. Previously published in *Ha-Olam*, issue 41 (October 20, 1931), 825.
6   Ps. 74:6.
7   The river flowing through Lutsk, a city near Trochenbrod.
8   Pejorative antisemitic term for Jews in some Slavic languages, including Ukrainian.

Screeching doors and shutters transmitted horrifying sounds,
>> Terrified faces hung in the window,
>> A pair of eyes met another pair—
Shabbat sleep disturbed by frightening angels of destruction....[9]

The sons of Haydamak[10] burst into the Jews' homes,
>> Their mouths spewing spiteful bile,
>> And like fire bursting in dark nights their
Rage conflagrating and their voices petrifying:

"Hey indolent to hell with you all! Hurry! Hustle!
>> Hasten! Get dressed, you sons of bitches!"—
>> Chased by the fear of crops
The Jews draped their backs with their weekday rags.

A sleepless flock all hustled, among them young and old
>> And the lad and maiden and pregnant
>> Streamed to the place of work—
Skies blushing with shame appeared on the horizon...

A woman was dragged her baby's mouth still at her breast:
>> His hunger not yet satisfied
>> The tormentor invaded her home,
With no mercy they chased her out with her little son.

---

9   A Talmudic expression.
10 Ukrainian insurgents against the Poles in the eighteenth century.

And among the crowd was a disabled man, limping on his right foot
> Shuffling behind the throng
> Leaning on his heavy cane

And his oppressor rushed him to run, thrashing him with his crop.
But one refused stubbornly to desecrate the Shabbat,
> The son of a rabbinic creed.
> Short, weak, and meager faced,

His heroic heart turned courageous by the fear and love of his creator.

And his soul became receptacle for the swearing and cursing his flesh to vicious thrashings:
> Beaten by the rod and shoved,
> Thrown around like a ball and dragged,

But took it lovingly as the old pure saints did.

On the Water[11]

My brothers reached the longed-for shore,
Landed on a solid land:
Only I remained on the water, caught in midstream,[12]
My ship is fully loaded with heavy freight.

I was late, that is; I was sure to catch up,
But meanwhile, night suddenly fell,
And who knows how long until day?—
My landscape is like a foamy sea, dark skies cover me.

A little flame winks at me—a faraway star.
With a thousand ropes my ship is tied to shore.
My brothers send smiling greetings from the other side,
There they had already ignited a tower of light . . .

---

11 From the collection of Avrom Bendavid-Val; translated from Yiddish by Andrew Cassel. Previously published in the *Mezryczer Trybune*, issue 39 (October 6, 1930), 3.

12 It is not clear which event triggered this poem. In October 1930, following the 1929 Arab riots in Palestine, the British mandate restricted immigration and resettlement of Jews in Palestine. The revolution of Oct. 24, 1930 in Brazil and the consequent rise of a nationalist government restricted immigration to Brazil. At that time Beider already had siblings in Brazil. His youngest brother Yomtov Hagai did not immigrate to Palestine until 1932.

In a Foreign Land[13]

My stepmother Poland spewed me out with spiteful deceits
Towards turbulent oceans and towering volcanoes:
To infinitely vast distances of remote Brazilian prairies,[14]
To the shores of the Amazon, which flows through *selva*[15] jungles.

My days and nights drift chasing something wondrous
On the Andes tall peaks and savannas—but all in vain:
Wild emptiness covers enormous tracts of land
My heart is pressed by the yearnings in the vast drabness.

Every step of my foot is a struggle,
A Roman gladiator's fight with wild beasts and foes:
Nasty predators in ambush, vermin and giant bugs,
colossal monstrous lizards the venom of serpentine *Rahabs*.[16]

The sun above is taunting me with blazing darts,
My back is stooped under the weight of an alien sky.
Tender dreams melt away beneath my sweating brow
Dreams of fine silky threads that my heart spun for years.

---

13 Courtesy of the United States Holocaust Memorial Museum—The Israel Beider collection.
14 Beider never set foot in Brazil where four of his siblings lived.
15 A tropical rainforest.
16 Biblical mythical sea monster; Isa. 51:9.

A heathen slave[17] I am, breaking pathways in my head[18]
Through primeval forests undisturbed by man;
With swollen feet I forge trails through barren deserts;
Sacrifice blood and marrow on a strange god's altar.

I don't recognize the god, nor does he want my sacrifice,
I cannot see nor want the mysterious in a foreign land.
Here I will wilt, a sapling detached from its nourishing roots,
Without a nation, without a God or a homeland's watchful eye.[19]

---

17   A Talmudic expression, e.g., Mishneh Torah, Slaves 9:8.
18   The original is not clear whether it is implying that this is just an imaginary situation or whether it means "with my head."
19   Borrowed from the last verse of the first stanza of Ha-Tikva which eventually became the Israeli national anthem.

At the Ice Rink[20]

Shouts and shrieks of joy
The rink is full
Here they fly on ice
Gleeful and exuberant.

An adolescent crowd
Joyous and buoyant
Cascades of laughter
Under a cold sun.

Pink cheeks
Beaming bright eyes:
Be happy little ones—
Now is your time!

---

20 From the collection of Avrom Bendavid-Val.

The Fair[21]

Alone, forlorn, friendless
I wander, lost at the fair,
My poem is percolating in me
Heavy with sorrow and pain.

Overwhelmed by misery and tedium
I stumble adrift among the crowd;
Opening a path for myself
Through a crowded pack of steeds.

Oinks the pig, bellows the ox;
Their voice tells me, "Be gone stranger!"
Where can I go to escape those voices?
The entire world for me is the fair . . . .

---

21 From the collection of Avrom Bendavid-Val.

Old Age

Old Age[1]

"Cherubs descended fortnight
Blazing, dressed in snow white,
The village lands' tarnished glow
Restored under a white dress of snow.

Pure crochet over myrtle,
Grove bushes and forest trees.
The artwork of a cold weaver,
Under my window is spread.

And when I rouse—a bright world,
All is pretty, shiny and clear;
A joyful wind wakes me up,
Steeping my heart with world's cheer."

II

This is the poem of a poet still young,
His heart glowing with world's gleam,
His blood invigorated by bubbling life,
His ears attuned to its sounds of thrill.

---

1   From the collection of Avrom Bendavid-Val.

And when marvelous feelings arise,
He jumps off his bed in a haste,
And runs out to the pretty leas
Covered in their new snowy dress.

And from his gentle lips
A blessing would emerge:
"Wear it joyfully my friends!"
And his heart glows the same.

III

This is the poem of a poet still young;
But I turned old long in the past.
The wide world, is so bright,
But not for me, mine is tight.

My spring is long in the past,
I too saw winter in the past;
If I look now at the world around—
It is no longer mine, nor its shine.

What in it for me,[2] flowery embroidery
Radiant skies or earthly curiosity?
By my window cold and death are calling,
I see them out in the fields dancing.

---

2   From Isa. 52:5.

IV

Morning by morning when I wake—
Along with the rage of old age:
I feel the beginning of my demise,
The days of my youth, oy, are winding down.

Morning by morning when I wake—
Along with thoughts[3] of bitter old age;
Shattered into pieces my violin is lying,
Popped the last of its strings.

Morning by morning I open an eye—
Which sheds a tear of bile:
In god's marvels I have no part,
All ended and finished so fast.

V

Where is my angel,
Who thrilled my heart,
Tickled my soul
When I was still young?

Where is my elfin-cherub
Who carried me on his arms
Offering me his splendor
His laughs and his charm?

---

3   A term used by Job 4:13 and 20:2.

Where is my paradise,
Where along its gilded paths
I heard divine sounds
Every day and night?

VI

Who blasted my violin
Silencing its songs,
Expelling the light of my life
Wrapping me in deep dark?

Whose hand raised
Sister, please tell
A sickle on my riches
Without any remit?

And hacked in my heart
My lovely yarn of dreams
Scattered it to the wind
Piece after piece

VII

When in morning, at the freezing frost,
Wrapped in shrouds, symbol of demise,
The ruler of all on earth and below,[4]

---

4   In Talmudic language God is described as the "Ruler of the heavens above and earth below," e.g., Devarim Rabbah 2:28.

Would squeeze from my eyes a boiling drop—
That is the tear of old age,
The decisive tear
Of countless griefs
With no solutions—
I will drag my feet
And hit the road—
With a bitter soul—
towards the hill.

VIII

When in morning, at the freezing frost,
Wrapped in shrouds, symbol of demise,
As He spreads his rule on all below,
Laughing a wild laugh, a scoundrel's laugh
Over the rotting graves
Of creatures and bloom,
Wilting chopped down
Under his blizzards' sands—
There near my hill
A brook gurgles
It mourns the dead
In enigmatic murmurs.

IX

The brook is crying for the demise of youths
The wilting flowers of myriad epochs,
Dreams that expired, songs that froze,
Froze in the cold.

The brook is crying in tears of old
Shed by eyes—that fell still;
In moans erupting from hearts' depths,
Deep like a void.

The brook is crying in violins' sounds
Struck tersely by a violent arm
Of the ageless old man—and ceased
Forever ceased.

At My Setting Sun[5]

Deep into my flesh the beast jabbed sharp fangs.
Ripping from me limb after limb,
My life's sun is setting, slowly-slowly dropping.
Only my heart is still sensing my awful pain.

My ears still hear the throbbing of my heart,
And my eyes still see my lifeblood spurting away—
Please let me sing the song of my life's last day,
Singing God's praise with my last breath.

I will not mourn a life that could have been,
And will not contemplate "why and wherefore?"
I will sing as long as my heart still flutters,
Until my eye's last spark and my final desire.

---

5   From the collection of Avrom Bendavid-Val.

Miscellaneous

Untitled[1]

Surrender your will to his will
So that he will surrender his will
To your will.
Yes—yes. I do hope
My time of redemption has arrived
You heard my cry[2] and you granted
My appeal.
God will come.

---

1   Courtesy of the United States Holocaust Memorial Museum—The Israel Beider collection.
2   From Jon. 2:3

The Jealousy Is Eating Me[3]

Like a pauper I stand by the river's splendor,
I have no plea on my lips,
And I carry nothing to please the water's divinity.
I am silent, my lips are locked.
I am the poorest of the poor.
Not even a sin that I can hurl[4]
To the waves.
I did not sin.
Why should I seek a pardon?
What really good it is—
But I do know that—
It is nice watching the sins
Of this community!
Because it is nice—to dump sins and keep sinning
Dump—and sin. And so on to no end!

* * *

Like cows whose tits are full[5]
When returning from pasture,
That's how you carry your own sins, wearied.
Oh, laden with iniquity![6]
And like cows just milked—regurgitating,

---

3 Courtesy of the United States Holocaust Memorial Museum—The Israel Beider collection.
4 Reference to Mic. 7:19 "You will hurl all our sins into the depths of the sea" and to "Tashlich," a customary Jewish atonement ritual performed during the High Holidays.
5 A metaphor similar to: "cows of *Bashan* on the hills of Samaria who defraud the poor," borrowed from Amos 4:1.
6 Isa. 1:4.

That's how you sinners stand,
When you hurl your sins onto the waves.
Point your kosher foot
In impertinence towards the heavens
And declare: we are innocent!
Oh, laden with iniquity!

Untitled[7]

> Don't despair my dear brother
> When in the west the sun has set.
> Always remember what I said,
> After night, the sun will be back.

---

[7] Courtesy of the United States Holocaust Memorial Museum—The Israel Beider collection and the collection of Avrom Bendavid-Val.

If for Each Failure of Mine[8]

If tears rained for each failure of mine
No dry land would be found to set foot on:
And not just Noah's flood would bring a covenant,
My tears will bring a rainbow too.

The zodiac wheel in heaven
Tilts when passing by my home;
If candles were my merchandise,
The sun would not set lifelong;

I work to succeed but never will,
Because my stars would turn away;
If I were a merchant of shrouds,
People would not die in all my days.

If I rise early to the ruler's home—
I'll be told he already left;
In the evening—he is already in bed.

He gets off his dray or lies in bed,
Too bad for the humble man
Born with his star dead.

---

8   From the collection of Avrom Bendavid-Val.

Ashmedai[9]

Suddenly *Ashmedai* acquired power,
Stole the king's ring and seal,
Darkened worlds with black demons' wings[10]
And he laughs ...
He has strewn Satanic laughter over the entire world:
He breaks solid, old tree trunks,[11]
He defiles old holy temples,
Burns in fires what man finds dear
Whose tongues of flame stick out, mocking heaven—
Ha-ha-ha!
Laughter thunders across the entire world.
Blackened clouds—endless hordes of wild-faced,
Black-winged devils fly
Red, dagger-like tongues of fire—
And all tangled together and danced around the demonic emperor.
The demon-dance grows wilder, hotter.
The bonfires' columns of smoke rise higher,
Demonic laughter thunders louder, tauntingly—ha-ha-ha!
The chosen man has given up.

---

9 Translated from Yiddish by Andrew Cassel and edited by Stephen Simons. Originally published in Vainer Ya'akov et al., eds., Ha-ilan ve-Shorashav: Sefer Korot Tal: Zofyovka—Ignatovka (Giv'atayim: Agudat Bet Tal, 1988), 238.
10 In the story of King Solomon and Ashmedai, Ashmedai tricked the king to hand over his signet ring whereupon he swallowed it and positioned one of his wings on earth and the other in heaven, and then hurled Solomon away four hundred *parasang* (פרסה in Hebrew, an ancient Persian unit of length; the European equivalent is League, about 3–3.5 miles), effectively deposing Solomon.
11 Another element in the story of King Solomon and Ashmedai.

Unclenched fists, silenced screams,
Mute lips quivering, unvoiced pain.
The cold plunderer looks on calmly, contemplating
whether to sacrifice another victim on Ashmedai's altar—
Golden treasures gilded through human effort.
Does man not care that his wealth is destroyed?
Doesn't man see that fire swallows quickly
His proud ego as well?
There are no heroes throughout mankind's settled earth,
Like those who arose in former days of Jewish history,
Who now could shackle the emperor of devils
In heavy chains engraved with the Ineffable Divine name.[12]
No hero in the generation of technology and sports
No Ineffable Name nor Word of God.
No God in men's hearts no genuine spirit—
Ashmedai's laughter thunders triumphantly:
Ha-ha-ha!

---

12 In the story of King Solomon and Ashmedai, Benaiah, the son of Yehoiada shackled Ashmedai with a chain engraved with the ineffable Name of God.

2

ESSAYS

Jerusalem. Image of the printed essay "Jerusalem." From *Ba-Derekh*, Issue 35 (August 31 1934), 3.

Jerusalem[1]

A

Jerusalem! You are the city of contradictions. City of differences, forever city of opposites! You are called the City of Peace,[2] destined as a secure homestead.[3] A small nation, peace-loving forever chose you for home! One temple for all nations, built by the King of Peace Solomon![4] Is there in God's world a city like you, a city of blood, battles and revolts, altar for massacres of nations and a battleground between countries and people and religions? Every lump of your dirt is saturated with blood: every stone of your stones is irrigated with blood; all your mountains and hills and vales and gorges are saturated with blood.

And your name is the "City of Peace"...

B

You are called the holy city. Divinity hovers in your air. Its echoes rise from your ruins. Gloomy hums emerge from your houses of worship, enveloped by an aura of holiness. Bells are ringing in your monasteries, sound of songs[5] from your

---

1 From the collection of Avrom Bendavid-Val. Originally published in *Ba-Derekh*, issue 35 (August 31, 1934), 3.

2 The name Jerusalem in Hebrew derives from the Hebrew word for "peace," shalom.

3 Isa. 33:20.

4 God chose King Solomon to build the temple because he never fought a war, 1 Kings 5:17–19.

5 Ex. 32:18.

mosques—too numerous to count. And all the sounds merge into one giant, holy choir, together they exclaim: holy! holy! holy![6] And these sounds hover over your mountains and fill your valleys.

Is there another one like you a city of defilement, filth, dung on every street corner?[7] And is there a murderer or a mugger, who did not set his impure feet in your wide gates and stinking alleys? Forever sullied with human carcasses, casualties of swords and famine and plague! Their stench and stink blended with frankincense burned and offered in your temples.

Is that you who is named "The Holy City"? . . .

C

Only a jester would call you the City of Justice. For there was no other city in the world where evil and theft walk erect[8] along with wronged justice, all within you,—Jerusalem. From the decrees of Antiochus to the tricks of Herod, the Romans' slave, the evil of Pontius Pilatus, to the wicked British rulers,[9] the present-day suppressors of Justice.

Look, they stole everything from us, the little nation of peace lovers, teachers of the world of the Torah of justice. [They stole] our land, our glory, our honor and all our precious treasures and they stole you too, the thief is within, Jerusalem.

---

6   From the Jewish daily prayers.
7   Lam. 1:4.
8   From Lev. 26:13.
9   The British rulers were mentioned in the original (handwritten) manuscript but were omitted from the printed version.

And none to take thought of you, none to seek you,[10] no one demands "give it back!" Isn't that a joke, heart breaking and painful, to be called the "City of Justice"?

D

Jerusalem! You are the most ancient city in the world. Each and every one of your stones is wrapped with the splendor of age. Each grave, every pile, every piece of rubble tells stories of generations that lived and died, nations that grew and wilted thousands of years past. Each ruin and cavern testify of a human culture that once sheltered there, until it collapsed under the burden of time or malicious blows. Archaeologists bear witness by digging in layers of your dirt. Your many wrinkles are evidence and the curved alleys and gates reveal your frailty.

But you are blessed with everlasting pleasures. Your youthful strength endures forever. You know the secret of preserving eternal youth. You raised the passion and desire of every nation and kingdom to love and cling to you, to sacrifice on your altar of love myriads of their sons and warriors. This is the fiery lust, which burned like fire in the hearts of heroes, renowned men thirsting to rule you: starting with Sennacherib, Nebuchadnezzar, Alexander the Macedonian, and the Roman Titus to the kingdoms of today—and so many we already forgot—you attracted them all, like a magnet, Jerusalem.

---

10   From Ezek. 34:6.

Undeniability you are the most ancient and youngest forever.

E

Jerusalem! You are ours. You were ours and you will remain ours forever. Despite all the historic murderers, despite those who defraud the poor who rob the needy,[11] who stole you from us not once—you are ours and will remain ours forever. Even if they stage, God forbid, thousands of pogroms against us, and even if they split us up once again, exile us from you by a wicked hand, we will certainly return when the time comes. We will cling to you and kiss your soil, reconstruct your stones and repair your ruins.

You are ours, our property, our asset. You are part of our identity, our existence.

You are like us. You are our symbol. We are united by the same adventures and the same attributes. Our fates are the same. We too are people of contradictions and opposites. We are a nation forever loving peace. We always sought true peace, even our greeting is [the word] "peace."[12] We pray for peace, unity, solidarity. Our prophets foresaw peace even among beasts.[13] All our books express peace and calm. But forever and to this day we scatter and divide into tribes, sects,

---

11   Amos 4:1.
12   The word "shalom," which means "peace" in Hebrew, is also the common Hebrew greeting.
13   E.g., "The wolf shall dwell with the lamb, the leopard lies down with the kid; the calf, the beast of prey, and the fatling together, with a little boy to herd them." Isa. 11:6.

factions, and classes, each fights for positions stubbornly until bloodied.

Also, what other nation in the world, which suffered every injustice, whose blood was spilled in every epoch like water, which quivered between eagle claws not once, is like our own?

We are the so-called Holy People. Our ancestors faced the true god, turned holy and passed their holiness from generation to generation. Our festivals and holidays are holy. Our Torah is holy. Our language is holy. Our land is holy. But alas! We are defiled at our fringes. Filth and refuse[14] are our lives. Every affliction and ailment buffeted us. Anguished and aching we are wandering and are transient among nations, becoming a villainy shame and laughingstock[15] for all the plagues that buffeted us from the day we exiled from our good land.

An ancient and primal nation we are. While Europe was still a barren desert, home to beasts of prey, our ancestors erected towers, castles and sphynxes in Egypt that amaze all their sightseers even today. And while Europeans still lived like primitives, walking around naked like Australian Aboriginals, ravenous tribes cannibalizing humans, we were studying divine laws directly from the Almighty on Mount Sinai.

And yet—how young is our nation. We are blessed with a precious ability for renewal like eagles. We know the secret of eternal youth. To this day our vigor is unabated.[16] Youthful impulses explode out of us again and again, in a powerful

---

14 Lam. 3:45.
15 Ps. 44:15.
16 From Deut. 34:7.

torrent. We are like a waking Samson.[17] And the nations, who left us for dead, wonder and ponder:

"Wherefrom does this ancient nation derive its strength untouched?"

Ha Jerusalem! Your fate—our fate. Your fate among the cities—our fate among the nations. That's why you are us and will remain ours forever and ever!

Completed on Elul 5689[18]

---

17 "She cried, 'Samson, the Philistines are upon you!' And he awoke from his sleep, thinking he would break loose and shake himself free as he had the other times. For he did not know that the LORD had departed from him." Judg. 16:20.
18 September 1929. A comment on the handwritten manuscript states that it was completed before the Jerusalem municipal elections.

The Modest One[19]

(Notes on Gelman's Character)

He trod the earth quietly. He walked along the side of the road, a modest footpath, as if he feared stepping on or disturbing someone. He did not have the necessary chutzpah to fight his way along a broad thoroughfare. In these times, when power belongs to the deafening advertisement, when the presumptuous pose dominates, when stronger elbows and military boots can push through the tumult and hoo-hah of life—there was no place for Avraham Gelman, the gentle, modest, shy poet. Thus his weak voice called forth no echo, therefore he painfully, alone and repressed, gave up his last breath before his time.

*

He was one of the modest, quiet, hidden saints ["*lamed-vavniks*"],[20] concealed in the shadows of life, like a pearl deep in the ocean, like a blossom in the dark secret forest. He avoided cheap affect, had no love for the harsh voice shrieking "I," lacked the audacity to display his riches in a shop window. The little wealth that he revealed in his poems and stories did not reflect even a tenth of his spiritual treasure and creative

---

19 Courtesy of the United States Holocaust Memorial Museum—The Israel Beider collection; translated from Yiddish by Andrew Cassel. Previously published in the *Podliasher Tsaytung*, issue 15–16 (April 24, 1937), 2. See image on p. 50. The headline at the top of the page indicates that it is a memorial tribute to Avraham Gelman, 5647–5697.

20 The Talmud tells that every generation has 36 (ל"ו) anonymous righteous ones by whose merit the world still exists.

ability, of his determined purity and multicolored palette. But those who were near him knew that he had a gentle, lyrical soul that expressed itself in a multitude of colors, which poured out together in a flaming rainbow of love, because love was all he had, genuine, beautiful and good, and compassion for the suffering. With his walking sticks in hand he went, chasing savage fate from city to city, town to town . . . . Everywhere his penetrating glance captured pictures of human pain and need, and his sensitive heart absorbed the tangle of human woe. From all his novels and poems, whether about a small, lost "sunbeam" that found its purpose in a tiny wood flame by whose light a poor girl read a book; or about the types of "old Międzyrzecz" Jews wholly devoted to Torah and the love of Israel; or only about the eternal estrangement between the "two worlds" of the poor and the rich—of everyone breathing with love for the noble, unassuming, modest; for those "quiet ones" to whom Bialik devoted his beautiful ode, "*Yehi khelki Imakhem*."[21] Gelman himself was one of those afflicted masses, those who, working and creating in obscurity, quietly without noise, neither demand nor receive even a thanks for their tireless work, and who are thus in truth the main pillars of a pure, honest, undisguised moral life.

*

And not only in his festive, creative literary works. The same modesty and love shone through his soul as well in his daily,

---

21 "Let my Lot be with You." The first two verses read as follows:

"Let my lot be with you, the humble of the world, silent souls, Conducting their lives discretely, modest thinkers and doers."

ordinary pedagogical work with which fate burdened him. At first glance it seemed that this occupation was a burden to the physically weak Gelman. In truth, however, it was for himself, for his spiritual ego, no punishment, no heavy burden that it was his fate to carry; on the contrary, only in the company of the 12- and 13-year-old *Moysheles* and *Shloymeles* did he feel fresh and free . . . . Only in that atmosphere did he breathe freely, honestly and in immaculate purity. Their gentleness was a delight to him and so he, more quickly than many modern, fully accredited teachers, was able to patiently put up with their caprices and "sins." His friendly relations with the students were not manufactured, devised, or done for show, but natural, from the heart . . . They stemmed from the depths of his innocent and eternally young soul. Many, many of his former students carry in their hearts today sweet memories of the gentle, faithful connection with "teacher Gelman." Many will have forever engraved in their memory the happy Hanukkah and *Purim* evenings, which they had the good fortune to enjoy in his modest dwelling, where they could feel at peace. And more than one tear will be shed at his premature death.

*

As lonely was his life—still more lonely was his death. A beam of light came and was extinguished. He worked until almost his last day, creating a new Hebrew dictionary. But he was not granted the chance to use it.

A quiet, modest funeral was for this gentle soul the last station in his wandering life.

Today Is Tisha'a be-Av[22]

Once again, the Jewish people mourn and lament the destruction of the Temple, the end of their golden age, their exile and enslavement, which has lasted almost two thousand years. And once again the Jew tearfully recalls the Jerusalem of old, the holy city, the princess among states that was despoiled and plundered repeatedly and that weeps all night, hears a comforting word from no one, because all her friends have betrayed her and turned into her foes.[23]

But it is not only for the destruction of the First and Second Temples that we weep and moan this Tisha'a be-Av. A fearfully sad feeling envelops us because of the new destruction, the destruction of the Third Temple, which might happen along with the projected [rise of the] "Jewish State." It might sound like a paradox, but this is how it is. Whoever has clear eyes, unclouded by [the zeal of] faction sees the danger of a new destruction creeping upon us, and whoever has ears hears the weeping voice of the Shekhinah, wrapped in tears and wailing by the gates of the modern Jerusalem, which is eternally being robbed from us. She weeps for the destruction of our hopes; for the honor of the misled Jewish people, who have been disgraced; for the victims who fell in vain to the hands of the Arab

---

22 Courtesy of the United States Holocaust Memorial Museum—The Israel Beider collection; translated from Yiddish by Andrew Cassel.
23 From Lam. 1:1–2.

pogromists[24] and for the treason that our friends, the "Bible People" committed against us.

Because a Jewish state without Jerusalem, without the Kinneret and Jordan, without all the holy burial places and mountains that are soaked with Jewish blood, without a Jewish people and without land on which to settle the persecuted Jews, yearning for redemption, suffering in their endless exile; a state in a territory 15 kilometers wide, in which a 40 percent are a minority of Arab pogrom bandits, with corridors for Arabs and Mandate-altered for the English colonial officers in the midst—such a state has no chance to exist and no proper existence and is doomed in advance. Such a state is only a joke and ... [original is missing words] Satan explain, to mock ... [original is missing words] our helplessness. Such a "state" ... [original is missing words] of our 2,000-year-old hopes [original is missing words] ... third. Because it is a resoundingly misleading name, without substantial content. Such a "state" is not a national home, but only a house of cards, which the slightest breeze will topple.

The coming new destruction will be more frightening and horrible than the old ones. Before those occurred, we enjoyed a bright age that lasted hundreds of years where Jews lived in *Eretz Yisrael* [Land of Israel] "each man under his own vine and fig tree."[25] We were a major power that ruled subjugated peoples. And after the destruction we could at least

---

24 There were two notable periods of Arab pogroms in Palestine: in 1929, and what was later called the Arab Revolt between 1936 and 1939. Because the article is undated, it is not clear to which Beider was referring.

25 1 Kings 5:5.

take satisfaction in our heroism. Our ancestors struggled and defended their independence and freedom to their last drop of blood. The Babylonians and the Romans paid dearly for our destruction. Now, however, we stand like helpless sheep and look on indifferently, while live pieces are being torn away from us, and we are ordered to pay levies, in addition to the robbery of land, to the Arab enemies at a time when we have not yet even begun to see the fruits of our superhuman efforts in Eretz Yisrael.

Then [the first and second destructions] we went into exile with a religious baggage, with a Torah, which for us was a substitute for a fatherland. Now we are naked, without an exclusively Jewish land, knowledge, or culture. We assimilate bit by bit, day by day among the various peoples, and every time another Jewish settlement dies, part of the nation itself is being destroyed.

Back then we began our path into exile through various backward lands in the East and the West and played a vital role in the world economy through commerce. Because of this we were in many places a respected element, which was favorably received. Now however, all the gates are closed to us. Wherever we live we are driven and chased out with fire and sword. We have fulfilled our mission, and the world no longer needs our commercial acumen. "The Negro has finished his job—the Negro can leave."

In view of the danger of a new destruction, worldwide Jewry must as one person apply all its efforts and stubbornly oppose the realization of this partition-project, which is merely a pretense for the annulment of the Mandate and Balfour

Declaration.[26] Our most powerful voices need to be raised in protest against the complicated robbery. We must demand that the world pay the debt it owes to us. The Mandate and the Balfour Declaration must be carried out!

And even if, God forbid, our cries do not help, we will have the satisfaction that we have fulfilled our duty and not acquiesced passively to the destruction of the Third Temple.

---

26 Ideas for the partition of Palestine between Jews and Arabs were floated from time to time. For example, one was reported by the Jewish Telegraphic Agency on January 31, 1934 (https://www.jta.org/archive/arabs-weigh-scheme-for-new-partition-of-terrain-of-palestine).

The Abbreviator, of Blessed Memory. Image of the handwritten first page of the story "The Abbreviator, of Blessed Memory." Courtesy of the United States Holocaust Memorial Museum—The Israel Beider collection and the collection of Avrom Bendavid-Val.

The Abbreviator, of Blessed Memory (A Khasidic Story)[27]

A

You must have heard about the "Abbreviator" of blessed memory. Is there anyone who had not heard of him?

His talking was always succinct. That was his strength. Those who understand the mystical tradition[28] tell that the Righteous from Belz,[29] of blessed memory, after blessing the *Havdalah*[30] cup on a Saturday night, and chanting "*Ha-Mavdil*,"[31] smoked his pipe and leaned comfortably on his chair's armrest, raising smoke rings to the ceiling, told that the Righteous from Grica of blessed memory, was the godfather in the Abbreviator's *brith*.[32] He sat on the father's-chair, held the child in his hands, and the *mohel*[33] was making his preparations, turning here, turning there ... and suddenly the following words escaped from the Gricer's mouth "Make it Brief!,"

---

27 Courtesy of the United States Holocaust Memorial Museum—The Israel Beider collection, and the collection of Avrom Bendavid-Val. A comment on the manuscript states that this story was published in *Ha-Kokhav*. However, this could not be verified.
28 In Hebrew: ח"ן - חכמת הנסתר, Ocultism.
29 Shalom Rokeach (1781–September 10, 1855), also known as the Sar Shalom (Hebrew: שר שלום, "Angel of Peace"), was the first Belzer Rebbe.
30 A Jewish religious ceremony that marks the end of Shabbat and the start of the new week.
31 "*Ha-Mavdil Bein Ḳodesh l'Kḥol*," a piyyut attributed to Yitzhak ben Yehudah Ibn Ghayyāth Ha-Levi (ca. eleventh century), it is sung during the Shabbat Havdalah.
32 The Jewish circumcision ceremony.
33 A Jewish person who performs the brith.

and the mohel immediately blessed and circumcised the child. To our group this was a sensation: How can such a thing be hastened? Where is the readiness [or getting ready] for fulfilling a mitzvah?[34] ... and then during the meal, he, of blessed memory, clarified those words: thanks to his [preordained] ability to be brief, the circumcised baby was intended to become the righteous of his generation. But up in heaven they were waiting until a righteous [down] here decreed so—and that's why they held up the mohel until I said something. And when I said: "Make it Brief," a special angel arrived, and turned the words into a frontlet[35] that he hung on the baby's forehead for all to remember...

And that's how it was.

His speech was always succinct. It could be interpreted in seventy ways. So what, where is the novelty here? "The Torah has 70 faces."[36] The righteous—is the Torah and the Torah is the righteous ... and people could interpret and understand his words however they wanted ... it's all true ... and that was his great strength....

And then one day his committed disciple Reb Moshe from Skole[37] arrived. And that you must know, all the Hassidic Jews called him "*Reb*"—Reb Moshe. And he [i.e., the Abbreviator], of blessed memory, said once about him "Moshe Skole is God

---

34 The reference is to a ritual recitation of "Hineni Mukhan U'mezuman" (I am ready and prepared) that is recited before performing certain Mitzvahs (e.g., drinking the first glass of wine during the Seder meal).
35 Exod. 28:36.
36 According to the elder sages; חז"ל.
37 Skolye in Yiddish, a town in the Lviv district, two hundred miles south of Trochenbrod, the seat of a Hassidic dynasty.

Fearing." And on another occasion, he blurted that "Moshe Skole is called so, because he lives in the village Skole and if it was not so, he will not be called by that name." His disciples could not understand that: What is he teaching us?[38] They knew that there had to be a deep meaning concealed in his words because he always spoke succinctly. They investigated it in depth, searched, labored and finally found the depth in his words. The meaning was as follows: "Moshe Skole is called so"—rather than the Righteous from Skole, as he deserved—"Because he lives in the village of Skole"—where he does renting and leasing—"and had he not"—the world would have recognized him as a righteous—and he would have been called the *Tzadik* (righteous) from Skole. And this is the true and correct interpretation. Indeed, he [the Abbreviator] had the ability to shorten....

Let's return to our matter. When his dedicated disciple Reb Moshe of Skole, of blessed memory, came to him one day unexpectedly, he left a great impression on him. He [the Abbreviator] even asked why did you come? It is neither a new moon now nor a Sabbath![39] Members of our group knew that he did not have to ask ... for all hidden matters were known to him ... he could just start the conversation. Reb Moshe answered that he is suffering a great deal of agony from his lord because a few cows that he leased from him died and the lord suspects that he killed them intentionally. Of course, one could wonder why he would do such a thing. How could it be possible? How could it be? But the lord does not want to hear

---

38 Aramaic phrase (e.g., Bava Batra 91a:10).
39 2 Kings 4:23.

anything, not even listen to an answer. He simply ordered to flog "Mashka" (that's how the lord called him) with whips.[40] And he [the Abbreviator], of blessed memory, interrupted Reb Moshe and said: "Go in peace! Oh well, hmm . . . a bull will die." No one understood these words. Those who understand the mystical tradition tried to suggest that the interpretation is: the lord values the cows because they provide milk and bear calves, and that's why he was so upset. But from now on, only bulls will die. So, what happened in the end? When Reb Moshe returned home, he was told that the lord fell ill. For now—when a quarrel lies and is delayed overnight, the quarrel is nullified[41] . . . the flogging was delayed, no punishment. And within a few days—the lord died. And so, they all saw what he, of blessed memory, meant when he said: "A bull will die . . . ."

B

He got rid of the lord—and a new king arose over . . . .[42] Initially, the new lord dealt with him with compassion: did not collect old debts, did not demand advances for rent and so on . . . . But all that did not last long. You certainly remember that: "It is well-known that Esau hated Jacob."[43] So, one day the lord called him in and said: "Mashka, go to town and buy me a top hat. If you get my size correctly, you will get fifty złoty and if

---

40 From 1 Kings 12:14.
41 From Aramaic (e.g., Sanhedrin 95a:5).
42 Exod. 1:8.
43 From Rashi on Gen. 33:4.

not—fifty lashes." Reb Moshe listened and said nothing. What could he say? He just went to see the "Abbreviator," of blessed memory, who lived not far, and told him about the incident. And he [the Abbreviator] replied in these words:[44] "So what, go and buy yourself a top hat." But the intrinsic meaning of this reply was not clear. Some interpreted it as: "buy yourself a top hat"—[that is] in your own size, and it would [also] fit the lord. But the truly knowledgeable, the ones who always can see the depth in the abbreviation, went further to interpret the depths of his intent: Get yourself a top hat that is made of silk or velvet and it would fit the lord as well.

And that's how it was....

Reb Moshe bought a velvet top hat, put it in a bag and brought it to the lord. Reb Moshe was certain that this was what the lord meant and that he got it right. Because just as brevity is powerful so is truth . . . because real truth emerges from real depth . . . the truth is always brief and it always emerges from the depth . . . The lord opened the bag and a smile appeared on his face, he pulled it out and put on his head the top hat of a real Polish nobleman.

Yes, good—the lord cried out—but Mashka how did you find out my correct size?

Sir—Reb Moshe replied—indeed the top hat is good, please sir, keep your promise....

Yes Mashka—the lord replied—the fifty złoty will be paid to you, but I am still surprised and wondering how you found my correct size.

---

44 An Aramaic term, common in Talmudic conversation.

Reb Moshe did not reply, because what could he say? How could he know what to say? He could not give the lord a simple answer.... Therefore, he remained silent and did not answer, following the rule of "conceal a matter"[45] ... and once he got the fifty złoty, he parted ways and left.

C

But the lord would not rest. After a few days the lord called Reb Moshe back and said: Mashka, I cannot possibly figure out how you found my exact size! My servants say that you simply stole my old top hat and used it to get my size. Therefore, if we find my [old] top hat in your possession, you will have to return the fifty złoty and will get a hundred lashes as a tip.

Reb Moshe was stunned and terrified....

"How could that be possible? Me stealing? I stole a top hat? And what else, of the lord's ... Hmm ... Absolutely long live Sir, go ahead and search ... and search ... and hmm...."

So, with an aching heart, Reb Moshe returned home and after a few hours the lord arrived accompanied by his servants, they entered the house, searched the attic and found it—they found the lord's old top hat. Without a doubt they themselves buried it under a pile of old rags ... the lord was terribly angry. He is a descendant of Esau, an idol worshiper, and anger is comparable to an idol worship ... and he issued an order to flog Reb Moshe. Reb Moshe dropped to his knees and cried

---

45 "It is the glory of god to conceal a matter, And the glory of a king to plumb a matter." Prov. 25:2.

and begged, asking to wait three days and meanwhile to put the top hat in a box and seal it. And then, to ask the lords of the region, his acquaintances, and friends, to come by and if they opine that the new top hat was measured using the old hat—he will accept his punishment.

The lord happened to be in a good mood at that moment. There is not a human being who cannot spare an hour... and he agreed.

Reb Moshe hit the road at once and went to see him [the Abbreviator], of blessed memory, and with a great measure of tears[46] told him everything. A hint of a smile appeared on the righteous' lips, and he said: "Go in peace! Didn't you buy yourself a top hat?" The meaning of this answer was exceedingly difficult to understand. Some said: "You bought a top-hat for him"—and therefore he does not need the old one. But those who truly understand said: you just bought a top hat—it is now possible to return to the hatmaker and ask him if you brought with you a sample top hat to get the proper measurement. But his heart would not accept it, only "The heart alone knows."[47] And those close to the table [the Abbreviator's table] said: you bought the top-hat for yourself, specifically a velvet top-hat, why should it remain in the lord's hand. This was indicative of an intent [i.e., you bought it in your own size]! Words of truth can be recognized....

And that's how it was.

On the third day, Reb Moshe got up early, took a sip of a spirit, recited loudly "By whose words all things came to

---

46   Ps. 80:6.
47   Prov. 14:10.

be,"[48] but this time he was referring to the words of the righteous, the Abbreviator, everything will depend now on the righteous... The righteous speaks and God does.[49] And so is also the reverse: the Holy One Blessed Be He speaks and the righteous annuls... That's the hidden meaning in "God is the Righteous..." as those who understand the mystical tradition know.... And then he went to the lord's house where his friends, the other lords, were already waiting, and on the table was sitting a sealed box. The lord stood up and said:

"Mashka, come over here!"

Reb Moshe approached the end of the table.

"Tell me Mashka—the lord said—when did you steal my top hat?"

"Me?—Reb Moshe answered—I never stole the lord's top hat."

"So, this top hat"—the lord asked—"the one which is sitting here—you did not steal either?"

"No sir" Reb Moshe replied.

"If so, where did this box come from? After all, it came from you!"

"Me? Reb Moshe answered—I don't know what was put inside the box."

"Let me show you what was put into the box," the lord replied, yelling in anger.

---

48   A Talmudic expression referring to God, e.g., Berakhot 40b:12.
49   Reference to one of the morning blessings: "Blessed is He who speaks and does."

He pulled out a pocketknife and cut off the seal, opened the box, and took out—a brand new velvet top-hat....[50]

The lord was thoroughly embarrassed and quickly turned it over to Reb Moshe.

And that is what the Abbreviator, of blessed memory, meant by his words: "After all you bought a top hat—of velvet for yourself, why should it remain in the lord's home...." And all of it succinctly, as he always did.

After all these events, the lord called Reb Moshe to his home and asked him to explain everything. Reb Moshe told him everything. After all, as our people would say, it is commanded to publicity sanctify the name of God for a miracle....[51]

The lord converted to Judaism and went to see him, of blessed memory....

No wonder, being succinct is powerful.

Międzyrzecz, Poland.

---

50 The box was supposed to contain the old hat that was found in the attic.
51 A Talmudic expression in reference to the Hanukkah candles whose intent is also to publicize the Hanukkah miracle, e.g., Shabbat 23b.

Rambam and His Gentile Adversary (A Folk Legend)[52]

In the days when Rambam lived among the Algerian communities in the lands of the Berbers in Africa his name grew famous. He was acclaimed and praised by all who knew him, and his opinion was respected and binding among the country's judges and councilors in the capital city who were members of the *Divan*.[53] Among them was a wise and mean judge named Pera,[54] who hated Rambam for quite some time for he was jealous of his wisdom.

One day, the Jews of the capital brought a query to Rambam about an open wine barrel that a gentile, a resident of Algiers, touched. Rambam ruled that the wine is *Yayin Nesekh*[55] and may not be imbibed [by observant Jews].

After a while, another question was brought to him: What is the rule about a barrel full of oil where a critter fell into it. Rambam ruled that the oil is kosher and may be consumed.

Some malicious Jews informed judge Pera about these two answers. The judge got angry about Rambam, his fury was burning and he said: Indeed, me and my nation are loathed and detested by these Jews more than the impure critters and

---

52 An undated clip from an unknown paper; from the collection of Avrom Bendavid-Val.
53 Tribunal or public audience room in Muslim countries.
54 The root of the name as spelled in this Hebrew text (פרע) is also the root of the word פרעות or pogroms.
55 יין נסך, a wine that is not kosher according to Jewish dietary laws because there is a suspicion that it might have been poured in a pagan ritual or an idol worship.

vermin. Therefore, he resolved to take revenge and plotted to kill Rambam.

Rambam found out about his enemy's plot to kill him. So he took all his personal treasures, gold, money and precious stones, put them in his pocket and rushed to one of the sailors and told him: My spirit is very depressed. Would you mind taking me out to sea on a tour to calm down my spirit? I will pay you whatever you charge.

The sailor agreed. As soon as they boarded the little ship, Rambam put covertly at the ship's stern the spell of *Kfitzat Derekh*[56] that he prepared in advance and the sailor fell asleep. Within a quarter of an hour, Rambam, his wife and sons who joined him on this excursion reached the shores of Egypt, several hundred Parasang from Algiers, where the ship stopped.

That's when the sailor woke up. When he saw the foreign land and people speaking a language he did not know he got very scared and cried out loudly, calling Rambam a sorcerer. But Rambam calmed him down by telling him: "Don't worry, within a quarter of an hour you will be back safely in Algiers. But you must watch out for one thing: when you reach the shores of Algiers and wake up, you must throw to the bottom of the sea the note that I put at the stern of your ship and be careful to never mention any of this to any mortal. Otherwise, trouble will find you and you will die."

The sailor promised him and swore to do all that. Rambam paid his fee and sent him away. And as Rambam said, the sailor reached Algiers safely.

---

56   קפיצת דרך, the shrinking of a stretch of land into a very short distance.

II

After a while, Rambam arrived at Cairo, Egypt's capital, where his reputation preceded him. The king's ministers extolled him to the king, talking about the wonderful medicines that Rambam used to heal dying patients. So the king appointed him as his household's doctor. And the king learned to like Rambam for his vast wisdom, knowledge, and good manners, and promoted and elevated him.

Word about the tributes and fame of Rambam, carried by sailors, reached the ears of his mortal enemy, Judge Pera of Algiers. He was greatly upset[57] and his face fell.[58] Three years later, on the occasion of the twenty fifth anniversary of the peace pact between the nations of Algiers and Egypt, the judges, members of the Divan, sent judge Pera to Egypt to recertify the pact going forward, as required by law.

The day after Pera's arrival Rambam summoned the ministering angel of fire.[59] And that caused a big outcry in Egypt because for six continuous days they could not light fire anywhere in Egypt and its colonies. The king asked all his wise men who understand such things to explain this mysterious phenomenon and they had no answer.

He also asked Rambam, who told him: "Long live the king! While I lived in Algiers, I learned that a judge there whose name is Pera is a terrible sorcerer, none like him in the entire land of Berbera. And now I heard that this sorcerer arrived

---

57 2 Sam. 13:21.
58 From Gen. 4:5, meaning he became upset.
59 A Talmudic concept of a divine entity that controls the fire, e.g., Pesachim 118a:21.

here to recertify the peace pact, but in fact he is plotting to kill you with one of his terrible spells and inherit your throne."

And the king said: "Isn't it the Pera who told me about you last night, that at such and such day and hour you fled Algiers because they were planning to sentence you to death for desecrating god and the judges of the Divan?"

Rambam spoke up and said:[60] "May the king live forever and protect his land from every peril. Is it beyond that Pera to plot plots and trap kings and countries in his wizardry and to spill the blood of innocents?" Rambam returned home and brought back to the king a certificate that was given to him by the officials in the Egyptian port on that same day that Pera claimed that he fled Algiers. He also brought the certificate from the gates of Cairo as evidence that on that day he was already in Egypt . . . and the king absolved Rambam and convicted Pera.

III

The king then consulted with his advisors what to do with Pera whose favor with the king was lost for urging disloyalty[61] to Rambam, the king's favorite.

On the eighth day of his arrival, Pera boarded his carriage, which was drawn by eight mighty stallions, along with his big and magnificent dog whom he loved and took with him

---

60 Exod. 4:1.
61 Deut. 13:6.

wherever he went, to travel to the king's palace to renew the pact and strike Rambam with his tongue.[62]

Along the way, an evil spirit overcame the dog.[63] Suddenly he jumped off the carriage and began barking in a horrifying voice and incendiary fire was blowing out of his mouth. The fire kept rising higher and higher until it touched the houses nearby as well as bystanders who were all devoured by fire.[64]

Pera was startled and frightened, not understanding what had become of his loyal dog. And when the crowd surrounding the carriage saw that terrible event, they became greatly upset, raised their voices and cried out:

Magician![65] Sorcerer! Catch him! Him and his dog! Hit them! Wouldn't you know that Egypt is lost because of him?"

And the people of Egypt jumped on him and tore him into pieces. And they destroyed his carriage, breaking it into thousands of pieces. And each one of them took for himself a little piece from the sorcerer and his dog, a small bone or a fingernail, or a strip of skin as a memento. And some took a shard of wood from the carriage. And the king's fury abated.[66]

From that day on, Rambam stayed in Egypt in peace and quiet for the rest of his life.[67]

---

62 A Talmudic expression; e.g., Sha'arei Teshuva 3:206.
63 1 Sam. 16:14.
64 Isa. 9:4.
65 חרטום, a magician-priest. See Exod. 7:22.
66 Esther 7:10.
67 Maimonides died in Egypt on December 12, 1204.

A Drop in the Sea (From the Recent Past)[68]

I

Those were clear days in *Sivan*.[69]

A magically beautiful night descended on the village. A nice and mystical spirit hovered over the houses that are deep in the greenery of trees and shrubs. A five-story tall mill stood there immersed in its thoughts, looking out through its numerous windows at the wheat fields gleaming in the gold of the setting sun, at the infinite plain, the brook flowing leisurely through it and the darkening grove in the distance . . . . The thick and darkish garden, which hides in its midst the priest's house on the hill across from our house, was camouflaged by a pale bluish fragrant misty air and was slumbering in a serene rest. The pleasant silence hovering over the village was disturbed only by the quiet gurgling of water seeping through the gates of the dam near the mill. Golden stars appeared one by one in the dark-blue sky.

I just returned from a sail in a boat, my lungs still saturated with the brook's clean air and my heart filled with warmth and pleasantness. I stood quietly by the door of the entry room with the oar in my hand. The wonderful view of the village

---

68 From the collection of Avrom Bendavid-Val. Published in *Ha-Tsefira* in three installments, issues 110, 111, and 112 (on May 14, 15, and 16, 1928); sections I and II were published as the first installment, section III was the second, and sections IV-VI were the third. The phrase "a drop in the sea" in the title is a Talmudic expression suggesting that this story is just a minor example in a sea of similar events.

69 The ninth month in the Jewish calendar when Shavuot is celebrated, typically June.

captivated my eyes and heart, I could not move. I was beyond myself. Nature captured me with its splendid wizardry. As if nailed to my place I stood scanning with my eyes from one side to the other.

Without noticing, my eyes got fixed on the tall linden tree on a high peak, which was standing out among the other trees of our garden that stretched out two hundred steps from our house. And then suddenly I was stricken by yearnings to a bird that used to nest in a hollow branch of this old linden. Last year, my first summer as a teacher of the sons of the local Jews, I used to visit that garden daily at twilight. I used to stroll until late at night along the path between the old lindens, listening breathlessly to the gloomy and penetrating songs of that bird.... It was a soft song of sadness, expressing a universal sorrow. It sounded like a heavenly voice vibrating in the garden's air, announcing a global grief. It rattled hidden cords in my heart, carrying me to endless distances, elevating me to infinite heights.

This summer I did not yet get to be in this garden. For the last three weeks, a torrent of robberies and murders flooded the entire county. Various rumors, one more terrible than the other, about cases of anarchy that took place in the villages and towns of the area robbed us of our peace of mind. For the last two days, there were frightening incidents even here in Reb Baruch's house. More than once we were raided by units from Petliura's[70] army who used the excuse that they were looking

---

70 Symon Vasylevych Petliura (1879–1926), a Ukrainian politician, supreme commander of the Ukrainian army, was connected with pogroms against Jews between 1918–1921.

for arms on behalf of the authorities. In lieu of arms, which obviously they did not find, they looted from Reb Baruch money and other goods. Obviously, all members of the household are now in constant fear. The house doors are locked with heavy locks as soon as the first star shows up in the azure skies and we stay imprisoned in the small rooms, suffocating with fear. But now I grabbed at the magic of nature and forgot about the lowly world where we live now. Like in a magic spell I was drawn here to enjoy the bird's song. I don't know why—but I truly love, particularly at twilight, to listen to a sad song that expresses yearnings, longing for something mysterious, lofty, unattainable . . . . I entered the hallway, laid down the oar, and walked to the garden.

II

The call of the master of the house, "we need to lock the doors!"—stopped me by the door. These words were said quietly expressing fear, sorrow and reluctance. I turned to face him and agreed. I entered the house with sadness and reluctance. My heart and my brain were still in the garden and with the birds. Only when I saw the face of the master of the house and the children's faces, which were marked with signs of fear, did I realize our sad condition. The garden with its rows of old lindens, its leafy fruit trees and the birds nesting among their branches were completely wiped off my heart. I recalled that we live in a despised world whose sunlight is redder than blood, and its air is saturated with the stench of human corpses. Wars, murders, pogroms, robbery, and larceny are now our portion.

Personally, I am not afraid, if robbers come at night—what will they steal from me? I have nothing that robbers may want. I am a poor teacher and I have nothing other than a few old rags that barely can be called "shirts" and a few science books that I keep in my trunk. But during the time of my stay in the village—for more than a year now—I got so used to the master of the house, that now I am being considered as part of the family, their happiness is my happiness, and their misfortune is my misfortune. And at that moment, my heart was aching with feelings of solidarity with their woes and fears. Reb Baruch locked the doors and returned home. I looked at his face, he looked as if he aged significantly in recent days. He is only thirty-eight but his face is already wrinkled and his hair is turning white. His eyes show fear and are swollen. In recent days he spoke little and even with his own household he is talking just the bare minimum while whispering. The constant fear robbed him of his joy of life. He is walking around gloomy, dispirited and sullen,[71] scared even by the sound of a driven leaf,[72] he would not be still at day or rest at night. He is deathly fearful at the sight of any unknown person, particularly if dressed in gray military uniforms. Indeed, his fear is not baseless. Aside from being well off, owning a mill and an estate with a field and garden, "The more property the more anxiety"[73]— particularly at times of anarchy—he is the only Jew in town, like a lamb among many wolves.[74] The peasants that used to

---

71   1 Kings 21:4.
72   Lev. 26:36.
73   Pirkei Avot 2:7.
74   A Talmudic expression, e.g., Midrash Tanchuma, Toldot 5:3.

treat him affectionately and respectfully for his generosity and wisdom—changed completely recently. An intense loathing of him started brewing. The venom of envy for his property started percolating. The reasons are well known: the beast that was hiding for generations in remote corners of their hearts was awakening from a long dormancy because of the war.[75] They realized that a rich Jew was living in their midst who is different in his conduct, his way of thinking, his everyday life, manners, and these differences are like a deep abyss between him and them.

Even now many of the peasants show him respect. But behind his back they bad mouth him . . . . Every so often they accuse him falsely of various misdeeds. Since early summer there have been five raids by soldiers on Reb Baruch's house. All instigated by peasants who accused him of hiding weapons at his home . . . . Although the accusations were never confirmed, the military men stole [from him] a significant amount of money, expensive clothing and houseware.

Since the first raid, none of us took off our clothes or shoes. We do not sleep like the rest of the world on a soft bed and sheets. We stayed up until dawn. Whoever falls asleep rests his head on the table and only at sunrise, if the night passed peacefully, with no mischance,[76] the children would drop tired on their beds.

To calm down his family, and possibly himself too, Reb Baruch hired three trusted peasants [to serve] as guards. They arrive every night armed with rifles that they kept since their

---

75 World War I.
76 1 Kings 5:18.

military service and stay overnight. Tonight, only one of them showed up. His name is Arkadi, a thirty-five-year-old peasant, bearded, gray eyes, smells like a pig farmer. During the winter Arkadi repairs shoes. No one knows where he learned to become a cobbler. But that profession earned him respect among the peasants. For whatever reason he related to Reb Baruch with affection, a fact that elevated him to be appointed as our guard. We all love Arkadi for his tendency to carry idle conversation, telling exaggerated tales, amuse us with his quizzes and proverbs that to some extent abated our boredom and desolation during the long sleepless nights.

The other two did not show up, and for unknown reasons, Arkadi did not bring his rifle tonight. We were concerned. The children started showing signs of fear, and Reb Baruch held back here for the night the three Jewish construction workers who worked on his new home. These construction workers are not from the village and usually they sleep in the barn. But tonight, they found a place in the attic. When I entered the lit dining room through the kitchen, I saw the three sitting and chatting with Arkadi. The master of the house listened quietly to their conversation; my two pupils, two lads 11 and 14 years old, and a seven-year-old girl, sat in the corner on a bench and whispered; the landlady, a feeble slow motioned woman and her older daughter, a 17-year-old maiden, were working in the kitchen preparing dinner.

With deep sorrow I took a seat by the table and opened a book. But I could not read. My heart felt as if squeezed in a vice. I was sad for being imprisoned indoors when it is so pleasant outside. How nice would it be if I could stroll in the garden with my pupils or in the field along the railroad track!

On the other hand, the current troubles of this household, of which I am also considered to be a part, burdened me....

Aside from the two rooms and the kitchen where Reb Baruch's family lived, which were to the right of the hallway, there was a similar apartment to the left. In the apartment lived: Baruch's father, an 80 year old sick man, who spends most of his time in bed; his wife, Baruch's mother, an old woman full of fear like a bunny, but otherwise healthy; their grown daughter whose husband is in America and her two children, ages seven and five; their two young maiden daughters, both over 25; and lastly their young son, Baruch's brother, Yosef, a thirty year old bachelor, partner in the mill.

III

And then came that terrible event that still makes my hair stand on an end when recalling it.

It was past eleven o'clock. The construction workers finished their dinner and climbed to the attic for the night. The children, my pupils, were napping sitting on the bench. The grown maiden was lying on her bed in the bedroom, fully dressed, wearing her shoes and snoring deep asleep. The lady of the house was still busy in the kitchen. She was slowly washing the dishes. Arkadi retired to a corner, sat on a chair snoring. We were three sitting by the table: me—at one end looking at the open book; Baruch and his brother were sitting at the right end and chatting quietly about the situation in the mill where work had stopped for the last eight days, due to the unusual events. Yosef sat for about a quarter of an hour and then got up to return to his apartment across the hallway.

He left—and while still talking returned, his face showing mortal fear and his eyes expressing terror. He quickly crossed the kitchen, while looking backwards at every step, and when he reached the dining room he whispered in panic: "we are leaving" and then looked at the door desperately. The lady of the house recoiled in an instant and with a slight touch woke up the three children who were napping on the bench. Reb Baruch jumped to his feet as if struck by a snake and ran to the kitchen door towards the hallway to face the intruders, but the children jumped from their bench and held onto his coat, as if trying to be protected from something that they only sensed instinctively without grasping it. Arkadi, the guard, opened his eyes but did not move, he remained sitting and yawning. In an instant a cloud of fear showed on everyone's face. I stood up in the blink of an eye and stood like a pillar of marble, but then regained my strength and walked a few steps. Partly out of curiosity and partly for a reason that I cannot recall now, I wanted to get to the door in the hallway and open it to see who was there. But I didn't even cross half of the kitchen's length, and Yosef did not get to answer Reb Baruch's question who he saw in the hallway—the door opened slightly, and bright eyes, like wolves' eyes, looked in through the narrow opening into the dark hallway. Then the face of a tall man pushed through into the partially dark kitchen. The face itself was obscured by the darkness, only his bright eyes were clearly visible, they were throwing sparks that wandered all over the room. A second later the door opened fully, and the owner of the eyes became fully visible. He took two steps into the kitchen, stood erect while casting his terrible stares everywhere. He was a man of about thirty-five years, tall and muscular. His tanned brown face expressed unusual strength and cruelty. He was wearing a military hat and dressed in an incredibly old military tunic decorated with shiny brass buttons and red stripes. He wore knee-high boots. He kept standing fully erect and without a word kept shooting his penetrating stares in every direction. His stares hit us in the blink of an eye. We stood in the dining room, by the kitchen door, nailed to the floor like silent statues while his stares kept aiming at us. This was a moment of mortal fear that felt like eternity. Then after realizing that there was no one else in the kitchen, he walked to the dining room door, where we stood, stuck his head into the room, his eyes searching every corner. Then he returned to the hallway walking fast, confidently and decisively, leaving the door open.

There was no need to speculate much about the character of this unpleasant person, what he wanted and how he entered through the doors that were locked with heavy iron locks. The sobering impression of his unexpected visit spoke for itself. It was clear that his visit was related to the incidents of robbery and murder that were rumored to have taken place in the area for the last two or three weeks. We did not even have time to think. Within a minute the visitor returned with a shiny handgun in one of his hands, its muzzle pointing at us. Now he quickly crossed the kitchen, there were sounds of people whispering, heavy boots stepping on the floor, and soon several other armed military men entered.

The first, probably the commander, approached confidently the master of the house and in a quiet tone of a commander said:

"You all go to the other apartment across the hallway!"

Reb Baruch tried to ask something quietly, but that man cut him off and calmly repeated his first order.

"You all go to the other apartment across the hallway!"

And as he was saying these words, he motioned with his hand towards that apartment while raising his handgun in the other hand to threaten us. That was a sufficient answer to the questions that were running through the minds of each one of us, and particularly to the question "why?" His wordless answer just augmented the fear that was crawling through our spines. Neither one of us could get to the bottom of the robber's mind and understand the purpose of his order to go over to the other apartment. We had no doubt that the robbers only wanted money and once we fulfilled their wishes our lives would be spared. The master of the house had already decided that if time comes, he will surrender all his possessions as a ransom for his entire family. But the order to leave our own apartment seemed to be incomprehensible. And this confusion just intensified our fear of the unknown of what might be coming in a few moments.

The master of the house stood shaking like a leaf driven in the wind. One could hear the children's teeth chattering while hanging with their fingernails to their father's coat. Their faces distorted with fear. Their eyes expressed an indescribable sadness. My older pupil, the fourteen-year-old boy, bit his lower lip. It was clear he was fighting a scream that was ready to escape through his mouth—but in vain: the crying and screaming that were building in the children's throats burst out suddenly shaking up the air. The little girl was the first to cry. She could not understand with her child's mind the danger of raising her voice with cries while robbers armed with rifles and handguns were facing us. Then the cries also emerged from her two brothers. The sounds combined to pierce the heavy silence. But all that lasted only a moment. The hand motion of the chief robber followed by a piercing look like a wild beast, which was getting ready to jump on its prey, restored the quiet in the room. But to emphasize, he blurted through his thick lips only one word in a quiet and commanding voice:

"Silence! . . . ."

The polished handgun kept hovering over our heads like the beak of a hawk hovering over chicks . . . . We all surrendered to the sight of the handgun. All the house residents, including Arkadi the guard, started to move, obeying the robbers' order. Out of confusion, they forgot about the older daughter who was sleeping in the bedroom. It appears like the effect of the spectacle on me was not as serious as on the rest of the people. Despite being agitated, I remembered that we could not leave the older daughter in the robbers' hands. I turned towards the bedroom to wake her up. But the robber stopped me and pushed me with his strong hand back to the kitchen. His push was so hard that I fell and rolled twice like a ball. As I was falling, I grabbed the leg of a shaky chair that held a samovar and cups. The chair rolled over and the dishes fell crashing loudly on the floor. Hearing the crashing dishes, the young maiden woke up startled, jumped half naked off her bed, and rushed to the kitchen. Her sleepy eyes expressed surprise and fear, her face ashen like a dead person. I was on the floor for a moment but seeing the robbers I tried to stand up. My heartbeat was rushing faster and faster. My arms and legs trembling, my joints loose, I dragged myself following the exiles.

Accompanied by three robbers, we walked like prisoners through the dark hallway to the other apartment (a fourth robber remained in the kitchen as a guard). The robbers walked in front and behind us with their rifles pointing at us. It was a terrible sight, it felt to me like a nightmare, like the horror images one can see in the cinema in a dark theater.

IV

We all entered the center room of the other apartment. The residents of that apartment, women and children joined us. My master's dad, who only rarely gets out of his bed, was spared by the robbers and remained in his bed. Our room was mostly dark. It was illuminated by light from the adjacent room, where the old man was lying, and which was illuminated by a lamp. The head of the robbers ordered us to sit on the beds in that room. The women and children surrendered to their orders but we, the men, remained standing, waiting for our fate. Then the chief turned to Reb Baruch:

"Master of the house, you have weapons in this house, turn them over to me...."

We were already used to this script. Military men arrived more than once, following the authority's orders, to look for weapons in Reb Baruch's home. But that was always during the day, in the presence of the homeowner, who was ordered to open all the closets and trunks. Indeed, at the end of the search the military men always took money and clothes; but we were already used to that. But now, a sudden attack in the middle of the night; removal from our apartment; threats with a handgun, the terrible stares—they all depressed the wretched and broken master of the house. A torrent of tears broke out of his eyes, like from a child's eyes, he tried to prove and beg, that he was clear of such an accusation, that there was no weapon in his house and that there never was any.

And when the women and children saw Reb Baruch cry, they too started crying and their loud voices shook the air. Yosef was quick to offer the chief a set of keys and suggested he should look wherever he wanted. He even offered to walk with him to show him around. But the robber angrily threw the keys to the floor. His stare was ice cold. The tears streaming from everybody's eyes would not soften his stone-hard heart. His eyes were firing blazing sparks, his face hard and angry. He tried but could not stop the screaming. He motioned towards his two aides. They stood up and aimed their rifles at us. The chief ordered in anger:

"Shush!—If you don't get quiet, I will order to shoot..."

But that did not help either. The children and the women who were losing their minds could not stop their tears. My little pupil, Sheindelle, cried the most. Two rivers of tears were streaming over her cheeks from her two black eyes, and shrieks were coming out of her little mouth:

"Daddy! Mommy!..."

Meanwhile I approached the wall and leaned on it while still standing. My heart was pounding. Something weighed on my mind like lead. My legs felt very tired, and they were slowly collapsing. My entire body was shaking like a fevered man. With a significant effort I raised my hand and pressed it to my chest, as if trying to stop with my hand the quivering of my heart. My senses felt like they were gone. My ears heard the whining of the women and children, my eyes saw the robbers pointing the muzzles of the rifles towards the master of the house.

And suddenly I heard the explosion of gunfire—and I fell to the ground—

I have several memories emerging from a fog with no connection between them and the events of that terrible night. The sound of the shot . . . . A terrible scream . . . . Chaos . . . . Voices crying "Help!" . . . . And then everything merged into one: the voices and the people became one terrible mass that streamed and flowed like a sudden flood . . . and then it turned into a terrible dark . . . . And the dark disappeared too . . . leaving behind nothing, empty space, an infinite void . . .

V

When I came to my senses, the eastern horizon was turning grey. The room was quiet. I heard the old man moaning in the adjacent room. My memory came back slowly. I was surprised by the quiet in the room. No one was there. With my remaining strength I got up and walked slowly to the old man's room that was lit. From him I learned that the intruders were gone, and everybody was in Reb Baruch's apartment. Unable to walk I crawled there on all fours. When I got there, I learned that Reb Baruch was seriously wounded but that his life was not in danger; the robbers stole money and clothes. But they left the house thinking that Reb Baruch was killed. That saved him.

VI

After an hour when the eastern horizon turned red, two peasant wagons stood by the house. The wounded Reb Baruch was lying on a pile of pillows on one of the wagons, pale like a dead man. The women, children and the old man were sitting on the other. Yosef decided to walk on foot. Reb Baruch's family decided to leave the village and move to the nearby town, ten parasang away. There at least, explained the old woman, Reb Baruch's mother, we will be living among Jews. Whatever happens to them will also happen to us.

I took my place on the platform near Arkadi who drove my master's wagon.

The first rays of the rising sun were dancing over the church's crosses when the wagons left the village. Sparrows were singing hymns to the new sun.

After taking a parting look at the brook, the mill, the wheat fields in the infinite plain, my last glance rested on the old linden, which was rising from Reb Baruch's Garden, and in whose hollow branch nested my bird, the sad poet.

—Farewell my bird! My lips whispered and my eyes welled with tears.

Without Bialik[77]

I am among those who were not fortunate to meet the greatest Hebrew poet face to face; I did not spend even a moment in his presence to be directly influenced by the intellectual luminosity that emanated from him. To me the name Bialik became over time an abstract spiritual term, a symbol of the Hebrew poetry....

I was jealous whenever I met a person that was fortunate to see him. Is that a small thing? A person who was lucky enough to see the wonderful poet with his own eyes, hear his words, look into his eyes, the penetrating eyes of a prophet who sees everything. That person must have gotten some of the poet's nobleness because he must have absorbed indirectly a supreme spiritual illumination from the rays of his glory, absorbed in .... [two sentences missing]

Nevertheless, I felt very close to him. I would not err or exaggerate by saying that from the day I learned his first poem, not two days would pass without me mentioning his name in a thought or a speech, when reading, writing, singing, or conversing with friends, at a time of sorrow or time of joy—the name Hayim Nahman Bialik was wondrously woven into the fabric of my life. At times he would even appear in my dreams....

***

---

[77] From the collection of Avrom Bendavid-Val; first published in *Ba-Derekh*, issue 33 (August 17, 1934), 3–4. The article is missing from the archived issue but it is listed in its Table of Contents.

One thing that I will never forget.

I was studying at the time in a yeshiva. The holiday was approaching. The students returned to their homes. Only ten students remained in the yeshiva building. They were sitting by their open *Gemara*[78] books, humming their quiet hymns. It felt somber by comparison to the loud voices of singing that were ordinarily filling the joyful space. The quiet hum rising from the corners only emphasized the sadness. Unintentionally, the memory of Rabbi Yossi[79] praying in one of the ruins of Jerusalem came to my mind....

And then a strong and resolute voice pierced the quiet. It was coming from a spot near the arc where one of the boys (I think it was Shniadovy) was standing by his lectern and reciting forcefully:

"I was sent to you by God,

He saw that you were oppressed."[80]

All the boys stopped their humming, held their breaths, and looked at the reciting boy. He kept standing, waving his hands, his eyes sparking lightning and his mouth spouting words in clear pronunciation, all excitedly.

---

78 A part of the Talmud that includes commentary on the Mishnah.
79 Rabbi Yossi was a second-generation student of Rabbi Akiva who survived the deaths of Rabbi Akiva's twenty-four thousand students. A legend says that Eliyahu Ha-Navi told Rabbi Yossi, that he should follow the example of his teacher, Rabbi Akiva, who after seeing the destruction of the Second Temple found the strength to comfort those around him and rebuild. "Don't stay inside the place of ruin, go out into the street and impact those around you. Don't worry about them changing you, change them!"
80 This is the first verse in the Yiddish poem by Bialik which was published in the Yiddish paper *Der-Id* [The last word, דאָס לעצטע וואָרט], issue 48–49 (December 3, 1901):

עאר האט געזעהען
איהר ווערט דערשטיקט

These words hit me like boulders, got deeply engraved in my memory like tattoos. I was still a young boy, did not quite understand everything. But I sensed that something new happened in the world. As if by a magic wand it turned into a new world, different from the earlier and still related to it. Like the relationship between that divine voice and the ruin where Rabbi Yossi held his prayer.

This was the first time I realized the wonderous influence the poet had and I became inseparably attached to him. From that moment on I started studying his poems as if they were chapters from the Bible.

***

Bialik. There is so much magic in his name. This name became like an amulet for me. Whenever I evoke the name Bialik—my dormant and humiliated national pride arises. When I evoke the name Bialik, real tangible characters come to life in all their glory: "The Talmud Student," "Morning Rays," "The Blessing," "If you Would Know," "The Last Corpses in the Desert," "Glory," "The Scroll of Fire," and many more. Every poem— a bright star illuminating the [dark sky of] exile. A stamp of objective truth, with no coverup, is imprinted on each idea expressed by Bialik's power of expression, Almighty's stamp. He engaged every heart with that truth, convinced and subdued, tempered and deepened the national identity.

What shall we do without Bialik? Where shall we go without him? Who will be our torch to illuminate our dark path? Who will comfort us in our grief? Who will chastise us when we sin? Oh, we are orphaned, our grief is boundless.

A black dark void was left in his place.

A Jewish Heart... Memories from the Recent Past[81]

This was before Pesach 1919, in shtetl S.[82] Times were very bad for the poor: there was hardly anyone who didn't worry about matzos and other necessities for the holiday.

There were many beggars in those days. To those already receiving charity regularly, and saw themselves as having a "right" to "*maot khitim*" aid,[83] a particularly large number was added that winter after the war,[84] which ruined many middle-class families. These were now forced to apply for a "gift in secret,"[85] along with five or six families from the surrounding villages and shtetls whose possessions were stolen or burned during the cruel days of the war while they barely escaped with their lives.

Here in this all-Jewish village, which lies hidden within a deep, thick forest, several miles from the [nearest] train station and a paved road, life was somewhat more peaceful and secure.

Yet no "maot chitim" was collected. For one, because no one was available to collect it. Even among the wealthiest

---

81 Translated from Yiddish by Andrew Cassel. Originally published in Ya'akov Vainer et al., eds., *Ha-Ilan ve-Shorashav: Sefer Korot Tal: Zofyovka—Ignatovka* (Giv'atayim: Agudat Bet Tal, 1988), 482.
82 Perhaps the village Sofiyovka.
83 מְעוֹת חִטִּים, an annual charity fund that helps the poor with Pesach necessities.
84 The Great War, World War I.
85 מתן בסתר, Prov. 21:14. A Jewish way to provide charity without humiliating the recipient by revealing his/her identity.

households, the so-called *"gvirim"*[86]—there were no champions in existence—they had not earned a penny[87] for a long time. The surrounding woods were full of all kinds of robbers and bandits, who spread terror among the population of the shtetls they passed. More than one Jew had lost his life walking or riding to a hamlet to conduct business. The security of the local citizens consisted of nothing more than promises from larger landlords, who themselves were concerned about having bread and potatoes.

Secondly, the rabbi declined to collect "maot khitim" out of anger at the shtetl that had left him hungry. A source of his income was selling yeast, and when challah ceased being baked for Shabbat, he simply went hungry. No one else took an interest in the poor people. Purim arrived and nobody even considered what would be with the twenty-five Jewish families who were unable to have a proper holiday.

But God intervened ahead of the calamity[88]—and this at a time when few could lead.

In the shtetl there was a stranger, a young man named Blitman. Nobody knew his Hebrew name. He came here in the summer of 1918 from a city in the Kiev province, seeking refuge from the Petliura bands that had persecuted him.

Blitman carried an identification card that showed him as a student at the Moscow University law school. He returned home [to Kiev] from Moscow fleeing the Bolsheviks, who

---

86 גבירים—a Hebrew and Yiddish term describing wealthy persons.
87 The term used is גרוּש—a basic monetary value that was used in the British Mandatory Palestine.
88 הקדים רפואה למכה—literally, provided a cure ahead of the calamity - a Talmudic term.

threatened him because he had served as a volunteer in Kerensky's army.[89] At home in Ukraine he had been quickly tried and convicted by the Petliura forces, and at the last moment, as he was facing the wall with his eyes covered, he was miraculously rescued from death and fled here, to the relatively peaceful village where his father kept some money.

Blitman was about 22 years old. He wore a gray *shinyel*[90] and a pair of heavy military service boots that contrasted with his intellectual appearance.

His face was pale, emaciated, long and beaten. From his plain wireless glasses looked out a pair of coal-black, deep yet penetrating eyes that projected an extraordinary power. He simply enchanted the peasant village maidens with his sharp glances.

Blitman came to the village almost unable to speak Yiddish, because he seldom heard Yiddish spoken at his gymnasium and university, or even at home with his half-assimilated parents. He kept busy there giving speeches in Russian. But his Russian activities did not last long.

Convincing himself that the hardworking, small-town Jews did not think much of the Russian language, he began within a short time to communicate in Yiddish, both in his lectures and on the street, and with the girls who flocked to him like bees to honey and were unable to converse in Russian.

---

89 Alexander Kerensky (1881–1970), the leader of the moderate faction of the Russian Socialist Revolutionary Party, which formed the Russian provisional government in February 1917 but was overthrown in November 1917 by Lenin's Bolsheviks.

90 Шинель, a Russian military overcoat.

It didn't take long, only a couple of months, before he began to speak in a fluent, sonorous Yiddish, enhanced with folkish expressions and terms. Later he wrote summaries of nature stories in Yiddish for the Moysheles and Shloymeles, who understood not a single bit of Russian.

Over time a group of youths began to surround Blitman, "half and a quarter intellectuals," that is, those who knew some Hebrew and Yiddish folk songs or were not ashamed to sometimes go out to stroll on Shabbat between the afternoon and evening services, or merely have good time. Blitman's living room turned into a gathering place for the youth who wanted to enjoy themselves merrily.

In the long winter evenings homey concerts would be organized here. The windows would shake from the dances and singing. The gang would sit on cushions, on bare straw sacks laid on the iron bed, on the one hanging shelf and even on the floor. They sang various happy songs, tapping feet and hands, whistling, trumpeting and humming with wild, bizarre, madhouse voices.

Jewish men and women obsessed darkly, spitting with anger as they walked by: "*Tfu* to this demon! Such an evildoer!"

And afterward they would recount that the Jewish goy had a route to the "pope" from the nearby village, eats pork there, was a complete in-law with his wife and on and on; sins for which he would certainly burn and roast in hell without any hope of resurrection.

But this Blitman took on the mission of caring for the poor people, with matzos for Pesach.

"Children!" he called out to his comrades one day. "I have a great idea, and you must help me carry it out." Everyone grew interested.

"We must provide matzos to the poor people. Don't laugh, because for them it is an issue of life and death, and there is nobody else who would do it."

"Maybe you want to do this without a rabbi's *shtreiml*?[91] We will go with you, taking the matzo fund together in a red scarf," joked two of the girls.

"I'm not joking. We can put together a 'show' and that will get us money."

The comrades looked at each other. No one had seen such a show since the village stood there.

Blitman then remarked: "It doesn't matter that we have no real actors. I know a little about theater and I will teach you. I'll act as if I am drunk and that there will be trouble."

This was Blitman's favorite word. And when he said it, he gave such a look with his eyes that everyone understood that the thing had been decided.

Naturally, the group agreed. Several out of curiosity, to learn about "theater." Others even more so for sport.

The gang got busy. They got hold of a Sholem Aleichem's booklet, and Blitman adapted his monologue "An Advice"[92] for the stage. He composed a couple of racy couplets, and a week after Purim they had the "general rehearsal."

Then Blitman approached the gabbai of the shul and demanded permission to organize a show in the women's shul.

---

91 A fur hat worn by Hassidic men on special occasions (e.g., Shabbat and holidays).
92 Sholem Aleichem, אן עצה [A bit of advice] (Amherst, Massachusetts: Steven Spielberg Digital Yiddish Library, No. 14793, National Yiddish Book Center), https://ia802909.us.archive.org/16/items/nybc214793/nybc214793.pdf.

The gabbai, an old Jew with a gray beard, a wagon driver, lost his temper:

"What do you mean? What kind of *chutzpa* [insolence] is this? Bad enough you turn your home into a bawdy house, now you'd profane the shul, the holy temple?"

[Blitman replied], "Nu, and when the Cossaks made a barn out of the study house—was that right?—Will you be happy when the poor have no matzo?"

Of course that was not desired—and permission was given.

On Saturday night the village had an enormous celebration. People streamed into the "theater" from all over.

In the morning, Blitman bought several sacks of flour, borrowed an apartment and organized a matzo workshop. Not one of the semi-intellectual girls or boys did not volunteer a day or two for the work. Matzos were baked, not only for the poor but even for the better-off, for a small fee that was used to provide meat and "four cups"[93] for the poor.

Blitman himself spent the whole day making a circuit among the rolling pins, telling titillating jokes and giving out compliments, caressing or pinching the girls' arms. He excitedly fetched the rabbi so he could declare the operation kosher; in a word the whole operation was found in excellent order.

Blessings came in from the pious old women—and of course from the poor after he presented himself as Taki the *Trapniak*, a total goy but with a heart of gold.

---

93 Of wine, the minimum number of cups to be consumed during the seder.

One of the matrons said: "If not him"—she nodded her head—"who would remember the poor now? A Jewish soul is beyond any price. Not for nothing did the sages say: One buys his share of the world to come in an hour.[94] He will surely [have his share in] the world to come!"

---

94 A Talmudic phrase, Avodah Zarah 18a.

3

LETTERS

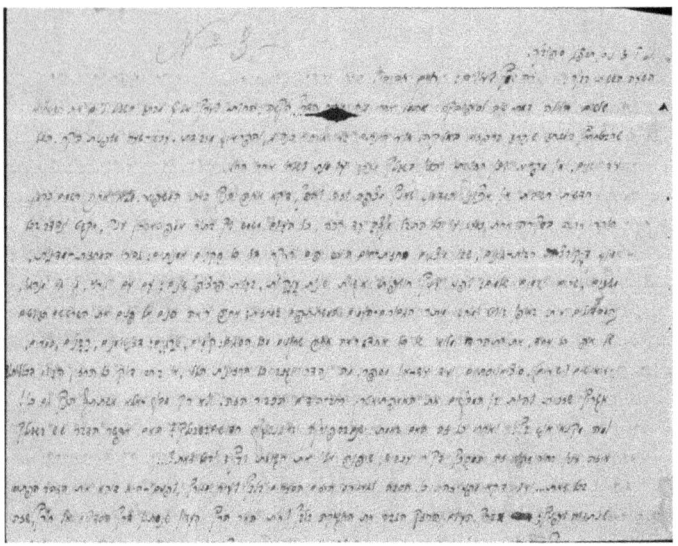

Letter to his Brother Hayim. Image of the first page of his letter to Hayim, Friday, 20 Nissan, 5683 Sofiyovka. Courtesy of the United States Holocaust Memorial Museum—The Israel Beider collection.

Letter to His Brother Hayim[1]

Friday, 20 Nissan, 5683[2] Sofiyovka.   No. 3
6 am. This belongs to the world [?]: My Dear Hayim!

Two nights ago, I returned to Sofiyovka. Yesterday, after recovering from the hard trip, I decided to write you a letter as promised in my letter from Olyka that I wrote in a hurry. But meanwhile, as usual, guests arrived and interrupted my work. And now it is predawn hour. Everyone is still sleeping. No one is distracting me. Therefore, I decided to write you this letter now that I will send after the holiday.[3]

There is no important news on our side. And I believe you do not expect any. Right now, you are the one who is making them. You are full of impressions like a pomegranate. You can scan the entire world from one end to the other in one quick glance. For you, the whole world is like a giant theatre, adorned with a multitude of colorful decorations, where the most beautiful real-life shows are being played without artistic replications; the protagonists of the shows are countries, kings, ministers and entire nations; numerous real giant personalities with various faces are passing in front of your eyes; each nation and its fate, each society and its habits, which materially distinguish them from the other nations—protagonists who take part in the shows; you see face-to-face

---

1 Courtesy of the United States Holocaust Memorial Museum—The Israel Beider collection.
2 April 6, 1923.
3 Passover.

the most prominent features of each and the full role of each; you also see actors of all kind: comical, tragic; gentlemen, rabbis, priests, Jesuits, socialists and so on with no end. How wonderful and majestic are these sights, or more precisely, the world in its entirety. You are fortunate to have been a visitor to this vast and enormous theatre! Not only a visitor but a participant! How jealous I am of you! And after all that, could there be any news for you in Sofiyovka or Ignatówka?[4] Is it even possible that you could find anything in this dark hole, which is covered with cobwebs, anything that would draw your attention? But still? ...

But still . . . . Or maybe despite that. Yes. That is the reason for your intense and passionate longing for your hometown for the sense of "once upon a time"—that bright glow that appeared in front of you; the intense luster of the world intensified in your heart the craving to the soft and gentle light that penetrated your room through the cracks.

[the end of this page is missing]

... quite a lot. But that does not relate to our matter, it is just because I wanted to tell you, that both Feige Rieder and your fiancé, who spent the last night in our house, because of the "ball," already woke up and are still in their beds chatting. I like both a lot, particularly Feige. She is so pleasant and gentle. Not only that, but her jokes and laughter, which are full of joy, make me feel alive. She has a lot of humility, and seriousness, but with all that she is also courageous and unbashful. There is no need to mention her intellectual development. Yesterday, after the "ball," they both were ready to hit the road to Ignatówka. It was 1 am. The air was full of wet snowflakes, which scattered

---

4 The Polish name of the nearby village Lozisht.

on the black road and wetted its soil.[5] The sky was cloudy. They were tired. They sat for the entirety of four hours in the tiny "hall," if not 4 by 4 cubits[6] then definitely not much more than that. This is the main room in "Old" Yehoshua'ke Leib's house. Imagine sitting for such a long time, crowded in the stifling air, which was warmed up by the breaths of eighty people, and watch these boring shows, without understanding anything, just sit and sweat—there was nothing there for these gentle maidens whose feet were squeezed into those slim "boats." And then walk three *versta*[7]—it was beyond their ability. I took pity on them and invited them to our house. Feige agreed after a brief discussion. Chaya hesitated and was about to decline. Only through an initiative by Herschel Klapke and his pleadings did I manage to convince her. They came in, took their shoes off their squashed feet, took off their upper dresses. Zlatka[8] fried for them some matzah.[9] Then I took them to the dining room, which now serves as a temporary bedroom for me and Zlatka, and I sat with them by the stove. I read them the Yiddish translation of *The Two Musicians* play. We chatted a bit and when we were done eating, we went to bed. I am in one of the rooms on two benches. Feige and Chaya on my bed that mother gave me.

[The rest of this letter is missing]

---

5   At the time of this letter, the roads leading to Trochenbrod and in the town itself were unpaved. A small segment of the town's main street was paved in the Spring of 1939 (Bendavid-Val, *The Heavens Are Empty: Discovering the Lost Town of Trochenbrod*, 57).
6   An ancient unit of length based on the distance from the elbow to the middle finger, approximately half a yard.
7   An obsolete Russian unit of length, approximately 3500 feet.
8   Beider's wife.
9   Probably *Matzah Brie* (or *Brei*), a typical Jewish Passover dish of matzah dipped in eggs and fried.

Letter to Hayim[10]

Hayim Shalom!

Your last letter of 17 Av[11] enjoyed quite a miraculous shortcut. It was on the way for no more than twenty-four days, while your other letters took more than a month to arrive. Must be because of your nice picture that was attached to the letter. It is well known to the Holy One Blessed Be He, that this picture can calm down my agitated mood, and disperse momentarily the signs of glum off my irate face, therefore He shortened its travel time. And my Zlatka, when she saw your picture—which is radiating beauty and loveliness—her spirit was elated. She already guessed for quite some time that we will get your picture in the coming days, and now she is displaying a face that expresses the joy of "victory" as if saying: "Aha, didn't I say that he will send his picture. I saw that she wanted to kiss it but was embarrassed to do so in my presence...."

In this letter from you I also found recompence for a letter I wrote to you in Sofiyovka during the Pesach holiday. I feared that the letter would be lost. I worried that its weight would attract the attention of the suspicious postal clerks, and that it would never reach you. I did not even keep myself a copy of it, despite pleadings by Feige Rieder, who was the protagonist of that letter, because I did not have the patience for it. Your thanks and blessings are my reward. Since I am in the mood

---

10 Courtesy of the United States Holocaust Memorial Museum—The Israel Beider collection and the Avrom Bendavid-Val collection.
11 July 30, 1923 (the date of this letter is at the bottom).

for writing I'll share with you one piece of news. The hope of getting some of my poems and stories in print has improved in recent days. The incident that took place, took place this way.[12] Shmuel Rosenstein who spent here a few of his vacation days, visited our home several times. As his way is that of holiness,[13] he likes to sit and chat continuously for five, six, and even seven hours. He is full of memories and impressions from Łódź. In one of those visits, he found me leafing through and reviewing some manuscripts. This work helps me forget the bitter present, so I do it often. His eyes caught a small but nice poem: "My six Happy Roosters!"[14] He would not budge until he read it once, twice, and third time, each time crying out "This is nice! This is excellent! Why wouldn't you publish it?" And he pleaded with me that I send it to the editor of *Ha-Kokhav* and to Katzenelson[15] who will certainly publish it, until finally I relented and promised to do so.... I already prepared several children poems but did not send them because I did not want to spend money on postage. What it plainly implies:[16] There are times I skip a meal. And at times I don't even have enough for one meal. But we will focus on that later.

And why was Shmuel Rosenstein coming and going to my house? Not just for plain friendship. There are [deeper] reasons for that. This young man smelled with his sharp nose that a nice maiden is living in my house. I mean our Feige Rieder

---

12 A Talmudic expression.
13 Talmudic expression, implying a sacrosanct routine.
14 This poem was not included in the present collection and was not found in archival search.
15 Itzhak Katzenelson (1886–1944), a Jewish poet and writer.
16 A Talmudic expression, e.g., Rashi on Gen. 8:7:2.

who came to visit us three weeks ago and stayed twelve days in our house. Not only that, but he also found out that Ya'akov Gorbatiy is courting her, in a manner of Jewish men. And he might have also found out that match makers noticed the young couple strolling every evening on the street whispering quietly, or find seclusion, under the cover of darkness, leaning on the banister in front of the house shaking up the area with their laughter. And you should know that Shmulik is Yankl's longtime enemy, hates him with passion. He cannot stand next to him and treats him like the dirt of the earth in his face and behind his back; and he is always plotting to hurt or damage him . . . . Of course the other side responds with abhorrence and hatred. In one word: these two youngsters always aim at hurting each other. Shmulik knew that Gorbatiy would not go to any place where he is sitting, and vice versa. He thought about it and came at three o'clock in the afternoon and stayed until eleven, the time when the strolling couple was normally due to return from their stroll. Of course, Gorbatiy standing behind the door heard an unrecognized voice, he peeked in and saw his adversary, and turned back in disgrace.[17] Of course he continued doing so day after day, giving Gorbatiy no relief for even one moment. Ya'akov would return to our home only after Shmulik left to return to Łódź. But to [Gorbtiy's] chagrin, halfway to Łódź, Shmulik turned back and returned to Olyka. He suddenly remembered that he had some unfinished "business" that needed to be completed properly. And on the following day, reb Shmuel was back to my home.

---

17 A reference to 2 Chron. 32:21 and Ezra 9:7.

That's how the rivalry over the maiden Reider evolved between the two young men. And you are certainly wondering: what does the "subject" have to say? The "subject" has nothing in her life but trouble and sorrow. After all we are talking about Feige. Her situation is very bad. She had enough of having free food in her uncle's home. In truth, she is now a grown up . . . . Her beauty is breathtaking. And she too wants to be independent; and here she only finds obstacles and critics. It is difficult for her to sit idle, and when she comes to [visit] me, she feels refreshed, full of youthful energy. She knows well that both Ya'akov and Shmuel are far from marrying her. The first for being short on dowery and the other for being too tall, much too tall for her. So, it matters nothing if she hears flattery from one or the other. Particularly since the latter is an excellent man and should be preferred over the former . . . . I wrote you all that to show that even at times of poverty and hardship, I still can find interest or a pal for idle conversation that distracts me from my poverty. At times I am so entertained and entertaining that Feige Reider and Zlatka hug me both at once, one on my neck and the other my head and kiss and kiss as if trying to fuse with me, bond with me. I never thought I would be able to attract such beautiful creatures to love me a boundless love. In truth, who am I and what am I, to be fortunate enough to attract Feige's attention? After all, I am a dry, tormented and denigrated driftwood, a man of pain and sickness, who has no form or beauty,[18] a man who is good for nothing, and even his livelihood is as hard to come

---

18   A reference to Isa. 53:2.

by like parting the Red Sea—and she is beautiful, strong, and everyone who sees her is attracted to her like a moth to the fire.

This is not the only thing that brings me pride and self-love, but when I get among intellectuals and educated people, I begin to realize that there is something in my personality that attracts people. I spent a year in the company of teachers in Olyka. And you must remember how I felt when I first set foot at the school's door. With how much fear and self-deprecation and meekness I looked at the teachers like a grasshopper at a person.[19] And how many times have you asked me repeatedly how the teachers treat me? And now, when I recall all that, I can only chuckle. And not because my heart became haughty over them[20] but simply because during the year I learned my own self value and now recognize that I am no less than they are, and now I look at them as one person to the other. The attitude of the teachers towards me could not be better. Even the [female] teacher Wiener, also Fisher and Rosenbaum treat me like a brother. I took part in all teacher affairs like one of them and always expressed my opinion without fear.

Yes, yes, too bad though that I am a miserable pauper. Only poverty can degrade a person, reduce and diminish him. A person whose fate is poverty is like a worm that everyone can tramp on. Yesterday I saw something that disgusted me. My landlord planted a vegetable garden on the lot around the house. In one of the beds within the garden, cabbage is growing and it got infested with worms. The landlord took a bowl filled with ember and threw the worms into it; they died after

---

19   An analogy derived from Num. 13:33.
20   From Deut. 17:20.

agonizing for about half a minute. That's how worms are [being treated]. And that's how a poor person is [being treated]. He is in the hands of the mightier and stronger who can treat him however they wish. Why am I telling you all that? It is in reference to me here in Olyka. I would have been happy if I had a small fortune, like all the other teachers do. That would have allowed me to support myself without needing help from ordinary mortals in Olyka. But I don't have it, and now I need to borrow or buy on credit and everybody knows that I am down to the last penny and would kill for one—and so I am as if I don't exist, like "a vessel filled with shame"[21] in my own eyes and in the eyes of my wife who lies in my arms, and in the eyes of all the illiterates who fill the market in Olyka. And I can see, even from far away, those illiterates sticking their tongues out at me and laughing crude and wild laughter. And I already can see how they are plotting to take advantage of me, sap my strength, my essence, and my brain, at half the price. They know I am hungry and will not haggle with them. I was planning to travel. Moshe David from Radziwillow[22] Invited me to come and stay with him. He would take care of me comfortably until I find a paying position. But the lack of the certificate holds this up. And the certificate is missing for the lack of money. The others, Fisher, Rosenbaum, and Weiner (the Polish teacher) have relatives in America who support them generously, and therefore they live peacefully and comfortably. When they saw that the Olyka people are malevolent in

---

21 A Talmudic expression.
22 Presently Radyvýliv, a small city approximately sixty-five miles south of Olyka.

their actions and mean in their finances and they no longer wish to support the school, they announced their resignation, spent huge sums and received the diplomas despite facing significant difficulties and obstacles and in the last three weeks burned through thirty dollars. Finally, they left this place: one to Bryski[23] the other to Zdolbuniv.[24] But not so me, I am forced to struggle here through epidemics, and enslave myself and my days, my essence and my strength for a lentil stew.[25]

Oh, how strong is my desire to take revenge on these crude and materialistic people, these ignorant[26] brutes! I wish I could witness that revenge, watch them crawl on all four and plead to me. Could you even imagine the extent of stupidity and crudeness that afflicted the Hebrew crowd like a rash.[27] Just watch and see. They squeezed the teachers for an entire year. They cut back every penny. They did not have any consideration of fairness, of the bad economy, the rising costs of all life necessities. Consider just a mere[28] thing. While the value of the dollar rose to three hundred thousand marks,[29] and the price of a pound of bread is five thousand, Mr. Fisher got 800,000. That is less than three dollars per month! . . . His salary was not sufficient to more than one week's worth of food, and he still ate during the remaining three weeks using money sent by his relatives in America! You would think that [the town's

---

23 A town in Poland.
24 A town approximately 40 miles southeast of Olyka.
25 Borrowed from Gen. 25:34.
26 A Talmudic term, e.g., Pirkei Avot 2:5.
27 A term used in Lev. 13:2.
28 Borrowed from Job 26:14.
29 Polish mark. The currency was extremely unstable due to Poland's wars with its neighbors. After 1921, hyperinflation decimated the mark.

people] are in bad shape, you would think that one should not be held responsible for [deeds done] while in pain,[30]—no, no. Just watch how these ignorant hagglers are throwing money on their rabbi, "let he live a long life."[31] The Holy Blessed Be He, gave him a son, whose time has come to marry a woman. The lad had nothing but his thick and fat belly, and his round face. He is lazy and tends the wind.[32] Do you know how much did the Olyka rabbi spend on the wedding? Twenty-five million marks in one day! That is almost a hundred dollars! Can you understand how badly leprosy infected the masses!

And after all that, isn't it clear how badly I want to take revenge on them? But there is a time for everything. I hope a day will come when I will be able to notify the Olykans that I had enough. But for now, I must sit quietly.

There are speaking babblers and there are writing babblers. Both the former and the latter don't recognize the ugliness of their acts until after their action. I too am wondering why I needed to bother you, the one who is so busy in his trade, with this "crude" plea? But what can I do? This is how I am. But I have a deeper reason for my babbling. I want to prevent you from fully distancing yourself from this life that you lived while you were still close to me. I want to bring you the thoughts of our life in general, the life of our nation in particular, and the life of your family "particularly and particularly . . . ." There is a great doubt that my words will be sufficient. But I had to do it.

---

30   A Talmudic expression.
31   שליט"א, a common blessing of Jewish clergy.
32   Hosea 12:2, implying uselessness.

There is no new news. Mom[33] will surely update you about her condition. I sent your letter to Shifra[34] and she will certainly write you as well. Feige Ridder left this house eight days ago. My Zlatka lives with me a life of sorrowfulness, but she loves me dearly. Our brother Shimon is in the "Silcys[?]" village. That's the reason he has not written to you all this time.

So, Shalom for now.

Yours, Yisrael.   Olyka   16 Elul 5683[35]

---

33 Bella Pearlmutter (see family tree Appendix B).
34 Their sister.
35 August 28, 1923.

Letter to His Brother Hayim or Hagai[36]

Dear and delightful brother![37]

Last week while I was in Sofiyovka I received your last letter of 7/13 of this year.[38] I could not reply to you immediately because I was a guest there for only a few days and from the first moment the "travel fever" caught up with me. Not only that, but another letter to you was already in my pocket, sealed and ready to go, which was certainly mailed already to you from there. I decided now to reply to your letter and particularly touch on the old question that you raised again. The question is: "Do I want to travel to Brazil alone, or together with my family." Indeed, my dear, you asked a difficult question! According to you, if I travel alone, I should be able to bring my family over within three months. Even if it was true, even if I knew for certain that I will succeed, there is still a doubt if it is worth to pursue such a big undertaking. I still have the ghosts of the world war's emergencies hovering in front of my eyes—those terrible dreadful spirits, awful and threatening; those that only five or six years ago[39] were real blocks, blocks thick like a wall that separated a father from son, a brother from brother, even

---

36 Courtesy of the United States Holocaust Memorial Museum—The Israel Beider collection, and the Avrom Bendavid-Val collection. This letter is undated. However, the text states that it was written "only five or six years" after the war thereby suggesting that it was written in 1923 or 1924.
37 This letter is identified in the Avrom Bendavid-Val collection as being addressed to Hagai. The context of the letter suggests that it was addressed to Hayim.
38 Probably 1923.
39 This suggests that the letter was written in 1923 or 1924.

if only three paces away. I still have engraved in my memory those awful days with live images of nightmares and scares, terror and horror, that turned our lives unbearable. A person would step out of his home and would not be sure if he would return. A person would leave for business to the nearest village or his hometown, planning to stay there for only two or three hours, and would not return for two or three months, after his entire household gave up on him for dead. You must remember what happened to our sister Sarah when her husband left her. She was a "living *aguna*"[40] and suffered and was tried by hardships and poverty. Why do I need to say more? We all remember the hardships and tribulations of those days . . . . We believe that those days passed and are now history, never to return, or at least for a long time. But still, my heart hesitates; I am afraid and fearful of traveling overseas and leaving behind my dearest people. Who would promise, who would guarantee that I will see them again in two or three months? And let's assume that it will happen, but during all that time I will suffer immensely by worrying for them and their well-being. I will constantly walk around gloomy like a shadow, immersed in depressing thoughts, full of worries that a difficulty will pop up, an unexpected obstacle will hold them up. And besides, Zlatka is delicate and soft, inexperienced in ways of life, never tried to set foot outside of Trochenbrod (her year in Międzyrzecz does not count), who will plead on her behalf? Who will accompany her? How would she travel through

---

40 Literally an "anchored woman." A religious term referring to a woman whose husband is missing and therefore cannot remarry until either her husband is found—dead or alive—or a rabbinic court releases her.

various foreign places, among aliens whose language she would not understand? Is it a small thing in your mind to leave Poland for Brazil? How many chambers of *Gehenna*[41] would one cross while traveling from here to there, until planting his feet on a ship's deck? How many toils of flesh and spirit would one bear? Traveling to and pleading clerks of the authority, they are numerous, and they cost a fortune. And how would little Zlatka from this quaint village be able to shoulder this burden? Particularly since she is the mother of two toddlers who are still bound to her and attached to her breasts.

And let's assume that I will not worry about that—do you really think I can get her on under Brazil's sky within three months? How will that happen? And where will I find in such a brief time the money to pay for her and the children's trip? You are writing that in Brazil I will find a better life, "particularly by teaching." If not for the serious sound of your letter, I would have suspected that you are kidding me. You must be mocking the poor.[42] How could that even be imagined? One can contemplate that after being in that country for a long time, after getting acclimated, after getting used to life there I might earn enough for a living. But in three months? Do you want to confuse me with a lie? I am a man of truth. I like to see myself as I am and not confusing shadows of mountains as being the mountains.[43] I like to account honestly for everything I do. And with all due respect, I can see that you erred as clearly as

---

[41] A Talmudic term describing seven chambers of hell. Also similar to Prov. 7:27 "Leading down to Death's inner chambers."
[42] From Prov. 17:5.
[43] From Judg. 9:36.

I can see my own mirror.[44] Loving me might have caused you that. Judge the situation coldly, with consideration,[45] with no sentiments, and you will realize that I will not get rich even in Brazil. Even you, well-shaped, elegant, healthy in your entire body and organs you too could not succeed in Brazil in the teaching "business"—I certainly cannot! As I know it, Brazil is not a country based on ideals, even less so than America. The Jewish settlement there is poor and meager. The Jewish population is spread out and scattered among the gentiles and there is nothing to brag about the Hebrew education in Brazil. And still the Brazilian Jew wishes to have his son recite the "*Kadish*" after his death, but in a Sephardi version. I am truly afraid that not one Hebrew teacher will fall victim in the fight for a comprehensive Hebrew education there. And you are telling me that "you will have a good life." Look how true is the German proverb "*Der Wille ist der Vater des Gedanke.*" That is "The will is the father of the thought." You are imagining what you want, even in this matter. But does this reality depend on a wish? No, no, don't say yes, my dear. It is truly clear to me and to you that it is very hard for a man like me to secure in life a strong position. This cannot be done in a matter of two or three months, particularly in Brazil where there is no vigorous Jewish life, but rather a sloppy and impoverished, still in a formative state. I should be lucky to make it there after two or three years of serious suffering. Indeed, there is nothing in this fact that relates to the core of the matter which would be the question: "why at all would I wish to leave Poland?" Most of

---

44   A Talmudic expression.
45   A Talmudic expression.

our family members, that is our adult and independent brothers, already immigrated and those left behind are planning to immigrate overseas.[46] Once our brother Shimon leaves to go there, only our younger siblings will be left here, and they too are harboring the idea of traveling that in the end they will execute. So what is there for me in this country? And why should I be the last? Why should I wait for old age when my strength diminished and my hope for a long, good life vanished? So I should say, there is nothing better for me than to move there while there is still time, while my children are still young, and I too have not aged yet, and I still have the strength to work and enjoy life. But what does that mean? [Only] when I can bring my entire family with me. Otherwise—it is not possible. In short: I concluded that I cannot leave behind all that is dear in my life and wander to Brazil alone. I am better off waiting another half a year, or more, until I can also bring Zlatka along. I think that during this time Shimon will manage to establish himself there to the point that he will be able to take part in the effort to save our entire family—including mom and the little children. You should know that our brother Herschel is studying to become a rabbi. And he is seeing success in his studies. He will earn his teaching certificate within half a year, one year at the most. This, in my opinion, will help a lot to improve the conditions for mom and the little children. And then, either they too will be able to move to Brazil, or, if they chose not to, I will not be too sorry for leaving them behind,

---

46 The family tree (Appendix B) shows that of the nine siblings, three immigrated to Brazil and three to the US, though it does not show the dates of their immigration.

because Herschel will mature by then, and he would be her support at old age.[47]

These are the things I thought I should say to answer your question. Please forgive me my dear for the extensive, probably unnecessary, babbling. I think you will see that these words are right because this is the truth.

And now I would like to let you know briefly of matters that relate to the lives of our family members. As I said at the top of this letter, I visited mom last week in Sofiyovka. I stopped there on my way back from Korets.[48] I told you of this trip in my earlier letter. I did not accomplish there anything, for now. But I did not waste anything either because my travel expenses of about 60 złoty were reimbursed. They want me there very, very much. But they cannot afford the price I am demanding. The difference is a tiny sum. But without that difference it is not worth me moving there. The negotiations are still not complete. It is quite possible that the matter will be settled favorably. You should know that also here in Międzyrzecz, where I was working for the last two years, they want me to stay, but expensive housing prevents me from staying. One can assume that I will abandon all the places, positions and "successful businesses" and move to Sofiyovka. That will make it easier for me to get a "passport" when I need it. -On my way to Korets and back I visited our sister Shifra in Rovno. She was then in the

---

47 In a poem included in this collection, "In a Foreign Land," Beider imagines the hardships of living in Brazil. On the other hand, in the poem "On the Water" Beider expresses regrets for not leaving Ukraine when he could.

48 Also spelled Koretz. Approximately eighty miles southeast of Trochenbrod.

maternity ward. She gave birth to a male boy. Congratulations to you! My visit made her happy. None of our family participated in the brith which took place last Saturday, Shoftim reading.[49] I could not stay over for the Shabbat because I had to continue to Sofiyovka to meet Zlatka whom I did not see for the entire summer. (By the way while in Rovno I also visited the *Iluy* [prodigy] who lives there. He asked about you. Do you remember his son Yosele? He grew and turned handsome, but he is an empty vessel, member of the Agudah,[50] loves to beautify himself, plays with his hair, trims his beard, and so on. The head of the yeshiva in Korets is Baruch Mordechai from Olyka, he is the Iluy's son in law. Do you remember "Yosel Maltcher," the one who used to sell the gemara books in the Zweihill [?] yeshiva. I heard something terrible about him. He killed himself by throwing himself into a deep well. He did it while insane, terrified by the secret police and army recruiters who came to town. He was convinced that they were all looking for him.)

In Sofiyovka, everything is like before. The Trochenbrod world is behaving as usual. Herschelle Klapka went to Israel and returned disappointed, after staying there for four months. Now, according to him, he wants to be "matched" [with a wife]. He is waiting until a nice and virtuous "bride" shows up, and most importantly with "cash." Itzhak Schuster wandered to Israel about a year ago and now he wants to return because his condition there is very bad.

[The end of this letter is missing]

---

49 The weekly Torah portion Deut. 16:19–21:9, which is typically read in mid-August.
50 Agudath Yisrael, a political movement of orthodox Jews who opposed the Zionist movement.

Letter to Hayim[51]

Shalom Hayim!

Trochenbrod's sun is still above my head. I still have part of the day and the entire night to rest here without work. Tomorrow morning, I will say goodbye here and return to Olyka. That's when my weekly workdays will resume. I want to take this opportunity to casually chat with you.

Last Friday, i.e., on the eve of the recent holidays, I prepared you a letter peppered with stories from the "city of wonders." I know you will be satisfied with those spices. But now I have nothing to add to those. No guests came to visit us during the last holidays. It is getting cold outside. I, too, hardly stepped out of the house. I was hoping that Chaya and Feige would entertain me at home. But that hope was dashed. There are signs of dissatisfaction on the side of your fiancé, and particularly her mother, about your trip to Argentina. Your mother-in-law said it explicitly to our brother Shimon when he visited her yesterday. It is possible that that was the reason why Chaya declined to come yesterday. But it is not possible to get away without anything.[52] Yoske Eisenstadt visited us several times. He gives the impression of a young German intellectual. Now he is attending the polytechnic in the city of Strelitz near Berlin. He is studying to become an engineer-technician. He told me about his impressions and about his father's life. He

---

51 Courtesy of the United States Holocaust Memorial Museum—The Israel Beider collection and the Avrom Bendavid-Val collection
52 A Talmudic expression.

visited Berlin while you still lived there. And had he known about you . . . but he did not. Herschel Klapka with Yurt's wife also visited us during one of the Passover evenings. Herschel, together with Schuster the teacher, now fills Yurt's role as the husband and suiter of his young wife. Yurt went for the holiday to Volodymyr.[53] And Herschel took the role of entertaining his wife. And the latter, as rumors suggest, fell in love full-heartedly with her husband's substitute. Even when Yurt was in Sofiyovka, she did not refrain from strolling arm-in-arm and showing in front of her husband her love to Klapka, which raised his [Yurt's] rage. It got to the point that she started resisting her husband on every occasion, just to annoy him. And when a young man came here, on Yurt and Schuster's initiative, on a date with Feige Rieder, the young lady started stirring up matters by talking the young man towards Chana Klapka. A competition ensued between the two ladies over the groom. Feige Rieder gave up at once her right. But Chana has not won him over yet either. And all thanks to miss Yurt who is an expert in raising strife and intrigues. I don't know why she came to visit us. Maybe because of Klapka, to please him. As for Schuster, as was said, he too fled to Volodymyr for the holiday with the excuse of looking for a teacher to replace you. It is not a secret that this is nothing but an uncertain and naïve excuse. The truth is that he changed his mind about "visiting" his "mistress" during the Passover holiday . . . otherwise how could it be explained that Mr. Schuster will make such a sacrifice for the school's benefit and leave behind the city and the things he like. In fact, I exaggerated too much by saying that I did not step out

---

53   Volodymyr, approximately eighty miles west of Trochenbrod.

of the house. Is it even possible to stay home? And although there is no place of entertainment in all Trochenbrod, I could still stroll on the street with my lovely Zlatka. And last night we traveled to Ignatówka to spend the holiday. It was late at night and all the houses of the hamlet were dark. Except my father in law's house who was sitting at that time and writing some "document." We visited him to allow me to say goodbye before I left for Olyka. What can I tell you? Zlatka likes me increasingly. Her love for me is getting stronger and stronger. In truth I am quite happy. I think she is sensing a pregnancy. But I decided not to let this thing "develop" and will use for now all means to relieve her from "unpleasant duties." This is an outcome of my decision to leave the country at some point, which will get harder with a "third" one.

At home things are as they were. Hardship is serious. No help. Mom is still grieving her loss of the rabbinic crown.[54] She thinks that all her other losses, like the departure of her sons to America, are rooted in this loss. Despite all of that, or maybe because of that, and maybe because of the quarrels between the rabbi who dominates in the village on one hand and most the village's residents on the other hand, she tried to bestow her "rights" on Eliyahu my brother-in-law, who is now like a "king without a nation." Now she had changed her mind. Our Herschel dropped to her feet and pleaded that she does not give up. He wants to become a rabbi who replaces our father. And Eliyahu, according to mom, took upon himself to teach him, for a fee of course, and he promises that Herschel will become a rabbi within three years.

---

54 Her husband Moshe David Pearlmuter/Beider was the Berezner Rabbi.

Olyka, 25 Nissan at night.

I stopped writing the letter midway. Meanwhile I left Sofiyovka and got here. Let's get back to the first matter. On Monday, mom troubled herself to go to Ignatówka to negotiate with Eliyahu. She returned exhausted from that trip and sad because Eliyahu refused to take our brother as a private student but wanted to add him to one of his classes and Herschel opposed that.

That same day a Divine Voice emerged[55] in Sofiyovka [saying] that through an initiative by the yeshiva students in our town, who also promised to help, a [new] yeshiva will be founded in Trochenbrod whose goal will be to compete with the school there [it is not clear where is that "there." It could be Ignatówka or Trochenbrod]. If that rumor is true, it must be because of efforts by my father-in-law. He talked to me privately and wondered how the Hebrew education of children can be entrusted in the hands of Itzikl the heretic. The head of the yeshiva will be our Eliyahu Ravitch whose salary will be 300,000 a month. The happiest of all about this is our brother Herschel.

No other notable events occurred in Trochenbrod. I will finish my letter here.

Be well, your brother Yisrael.

[A note in handwriting different from that of Beider at the bottom states: "This letter was written on the last day of the Pesach holiday this year. Started in Sofiyovka and completed it in Olyka."]

---

55 A Talmudic expression.

Letter to an Unnamed Friend in Międzyrzecz[56]

Dear friend,

I am jealous of you for having loyal friends that write you often in Hebrew. You even get letters in Hebrew from your son in Eretz Yisrael. To a great degree you live in a Hebrew environment, insofar as one can speak of a Hebrew environment in the diaspora. It is not like that for me. My brothers and friends have stopped writing to me for quite some time. Apart from my students' notebooks I see almost no written Hebrew words for years at a time, except of course for those that I scribble myself for fun.

So I thought that I should try writing you a letter. Perhaps you will wish to reward me with a written reply. And that will be my reward. But even if you chose to ignore this letter, merely writing it would be my reward—that is, the pleasure of merely writing it. Because I am sure that you, like me, feel a sense of caution and respect[57] when you write in Hebrew. After all, among us the few Hebrew speakers, Hebrew is like a religious ritual. We sacrifice our entire lives on the altar of our love to this language. Did you notice the unique happiness that bubbles up within you when reading a letter in Hebrew written in an elegant and clear style, where every period, comma, question mark, exclamation point, dash, parenthesis, and quotation mark appear in their proper places? I doubt if a

---

56 From the collection of Avrom Bendavid-Val.
57 דחילו ורחימו An Aramaic term often used as an introduction to a prayer or a blessing.

non-Hebrew speaker would feel the same when reading something in another language.

I would not say that such feelings bring respect to the Hebrew as a spoken language. Just the opposite. Undoubtedly such feelings, May the Merciful One save us,[58] show how unnatural is this situation. A writer in a living language does not have such feelings of love or joy. Does anyone feel love for the teeth which he is using to eat? Does he feel joy for his fingers that grasp a pen? Whatever is natural is often self-evident. I note this only to highlight that the Hebrew language is like a religious ritual for us.

Not without reason our fathers called it "The Holy Language." Not only because they used it often for holy purposes, places, and occasions, but also because they loved it and felt in it an inherent holiness, godliness, awe. One who sat down to write something in Hebrew felt a special emotion in his heart, that he was doing something above and beyond the daily life: that he would search for flowery expressions and idioms that ring beautiful. Even the handwriting was polished, ornated and curled until it rose to a level of art. Even the content was chosen as not to be derived from daily life. Often the act of writing became a goal all by itself, rather than a means to express ideas, because the writing was the essence rather than the tool, the language itself was the essence, the language of holy writings. And even us, as hard as we try to introduce the Hebrew into our daily secular life by removing it from the holiness, dusting off its holy dust, we still fail, and I think we will never succeed to free ourselves from that unique feeling

---

58   A common Aramaic term that is often expressed by the acronym ר״ל.

that dominates us while writing, the sense of "for the sake of unification"[59] of the Holly One....

But currently there is no respect for the language. Everyone feels free to grab a pen and write. Grammar is annulled: The *light dagesh* and the *strong dagesh*[60] disappeared; overall the rules of [Hebrew] nikud turned into history. Even schools no longer teach them. The refined style is now the exclusive domain of well-known authors. And the handwriting—who is paying attention nowadays to such a minor detail? Every letter from the Land of Israel is stunning with its ridiculous errors, and sloppy handwriting.

But no one is upset about that. Because this is a testimony that the language in our land is alive, that it is the exclusive tool for expressing daily life. While we, and others like us, are prepared to be killed over less than a *Shva Na*,[61] and derive pleasure from merely writing in Hebrew.

And now I suppose you will understand my reason for writing to you while living in the same town and seeing each other often. One more thing: it is well known that an idea can be expressed more precisely in writing than orally. Because orally words emerge in an urgent haste[62] without sufficient reason or explanation. But not so in writing. The writer is not rushed and is freed from inaccuracies that might occur in a routine speech.

---

59 Part of a short prayer that is said before performing certain commandments to express dedication and commitment.
60 Two elements of the Hebrew vowel pointing system.
61 A minor element of the Hebrew vowel pointing system.
62 From Esther 8:14.

Therefore, I think that it would be worthwhile for us to express in writing our various ideas and try to clarify for ourselves various questions with which our times are either blessed or cursed.

And that can be done only in writing.

I will be glad if you would accept my invitation.

Yours,
Y. Beider
Międzyrzecz
8 Elul, 5689[63]

---

63   September 13, 1929.

Letter to His Brother Shimon[64]

Kruszyn[65]   19 February, 1932
Shalom my Dear Shimon!

I received your letters, and as you might imagine my joy was boundless. I answered at once your first letter but for the lack of stamps I could not send it. Meanwhile your last letter of January 12 arrived as well. So I would like to use this letter to reply to both. I am extremely glad that you decided to start communicating with me. It is true, as you commented in your last letter, that I am not alone here without a kin or a redeemer.[66] But when I don't get letters from you and mother it upsets me to the point that I give up everything and feel like not only I am deprived of relatives but I am the only [remaining] person in the world. In particular I am missing a close person or a close brother with whom I can share my anguish that otherwise remains contained in my heart with no way of sharing . . . since mother left. I started now walking along a new path . . . . I realized that if I was to rely on someone's help or expect salvation from my distant brothers, I would not get anywhere. Therefore, I decided to transition to a life that will assure my survival. I was sure that the Land of Israel will answer my difficult question and my life there will not only be labeled as an ideal life but a [real] life, the life of a man. In the last two years

---

64   From the collection of Avrom Bendavid-Val.
65   Kruszyn is approximately 130 miles west of Warsaw; the letter explains his presence there.
66   A biblical term, e.g., Ruth 2:20.

I suffered great disappointments—the greatest disappointment was the realization that my *aliyah*[67] to the Land of Israel will not happen as fast [as I hoped] because the British government is damaging us by not letting us to continue building what we started,[68] but at the same time you declined to respond to my [earlier] letter asking for a boat ticket (that was my letter to you from Warsaw that I sent to Portugal). And so, with no other options, I had to continue along the [current] path, but that necessity further strengthened my belief in the implementation of the pioneering Zionism, my belief in collective life, and I keep to myself my numerous disappointments.... Last year I spent a few months at a pioneers' conference in Warsaw. That elevated me again to the level of a man who follows the popular—human—Zionist—socialist ideal of living in a kibbutz.[69] Indeed, life in the kibbutz today is hard. As you can imagine the number of unemployed in Poland is high—and if one finds work thanks to our pioneering privileges, the low compensation is insufficient to live on and provide the worker's needs, which are plenty. Add to that the frequent obstacles the British government is placing on

---

67 Ascent, עליה, the Hebrew term for immigration to Israel.
68 This might be a reference to the 1930 Passfield White Paper that was the response to the 1929 Arab riots and recommended restrictions on Jewish immigration to the Mandatory Palestine and land purchases by Jews. However, in February 1931 those recommendations were annulled by prime minister MacDonald.
69 Most likely it was one of *Ha-Halutz* training farms (e.g., in Grochów near Warsaw) that were established to prepare pioneers for their life in Mandatory Palestine.

immigration[70] and the personal vacillations and—last but not least the poor social life—it is so depressing that often one is ready to leave the kibbutz and return home. Only the expectation that soon I will be able to make Aliyah keeps me in the kibbutz—and regardless of the desperation that took me over, I am going forward and will continue while suppressing my pain and great disappointment.

Your last letter in which you wrote about your anxiety that is related to the latest "International" events and my own situation, actually reassured me. I now see that at the very least I have a brother who keeps me in his mind and did not forget his depressed brother here in Europe and without any escape route. But I would like to reassure you a bit by saying that I am trying to make Aliyah as soon as possible. One company of 500 person (keep it quiet) made recently an illegal Aliyah and another company, which will include me, is expected to make Aliyah soon. And even if war breaks out, that Aliyah will not be stopped. Of course, this depends on the success of the earlier company. Therefore, there is no point now for you to suggest that I immigrate now from Poland. If such a time ever comes, I will have to forgo two and a half years of a life of poverty and suffering for the sake of immigrating to another country. But for now, I am full of energy and desire to immigrate to the Land of Israel (despite having a disappointment with the overall endeavor). For now, I thank you from the bottom of my heart—and I recognize your devotion to me as a brother. I am

---

70 The October 1930 White Paper restrictions on immigration were repelled. However, the 1939 White Paper did eventually restrict Jewish immigration to 75,000 over a period of five years.

also full of gratitude for your effort to get me some money. On the other hand, I want to clarify to you Shifra's situation and suggest that you try to help her the best you can (don't consider it shameful for one to solicit help for others while he himself has nothing). The concrete help you could provide is to take upon yourself two costs (for her and for Yitzhak).[71] And when they reach Brazil, they will pay you back. I know it is not that easy, but you must understand that if you see this as a way out of her tough situation you must make that effort. Her groom promised to give her a few hundred dollars to arrange her travel to Brazil. I also got a letter from Israel; he is gravely ill. His words that made me shade tears were: "My life is in danger if I don't get into a summer home." What to do? I would also like to let you know that I got a letter from Naftali (I did not read it yet). He left the hospital—I don't know what his disease was. He is writing that he was left handicapped—limping. Do you know anything about him? And how about Zalman? Why isn't he writing? Congratulate him on my behalf. I hope you will not hold up your reply to me. Send it to Shifra's address. I am hungry for your letters. Tell me a little bit about the public life in Brazil and your own life.

I wish you blessings and a blessed life. Don't forget your brother and sister in the Polish exile. I bless you, Hinde and your daughter.

From the bottom of my heart.

Your brother Y. Beider.

---

71   Her groom.

Letter to His Brothers Zalman and Naftali [on the Death of Shimon][72]

Yisrael Beider   Friday the 7th day of Shvat, 569[?][73]
Międzyrzecz near Lukow

Blessings and peace upon you, beloved brothers Zalman[74] and Naftali!

I write to both of you in a single letter in reply to your two letters, which I received today. Let this be a symbol of our unity and loyalty. You suffer together in your wanders in foreign lands, and together you seek redemption for your souls. We are brothers in our grief and will be brothers in our solace. You are companions in being eyewitnesses to the death of our brother of blessed memory. Let this letter of mine be your joint solace. Because the two are better off when united than the one.[75] By joining the two of you with this letter we combine to become a threefold cord that is not readily broken.[76]

Yes, I too need the same thing, like you, to be cheered up and solaced. That is why my role as the comforter is particularly difficult. I am now like the man who is drowning in the middle of the ocean and is trying to pull himself out of the

---

72 From the collection of Avrom Bendavid-Val.
73 The last character of the Hebrew year is faded. The seventh day of Shvat fell on a Friday five times in the Hebrew calendar decade that started on 5690: in 1932, 1933, 1935, 1936 and 1939. A letter from Beider to his mother on April 2, 1935, suggests that on that date Shimon was still alive.
74 This is the same brother Beider referred to as Hayim in other letters.
75 From Eccles. 4:9.
76 Eccles. 4:12.

raging waves by pulling on his own hair. That is, I am grieving and I must console myself. I may manage during my daily life obligations to forget the death of my brother, but your wound must be deeper than mine because it was recorded in person in your memory. I understand and feel the difficulty of my role of healing that wound. I understand my obligation as the older and more experienced brother to cheer you up and strengthen you. I hope you will listen to my following words and help me drive out the shadows of your sorrow that keep chasing you and disturb your peace. [illegible sentence]. Let's explore the matter.

First: "The tragedy of the many."[77] The divine provided a cure ahead of the affliction[78] by making death general and shared by all living. On that day, the eleventh of Tevet, when I opened your letter written by Naftali and saw the black frames, I remained sitting stunned and void of feelings. I dropped on my chair as a dark cloud descended and weighed on all the rooms of my house. Half dazed by this sudden piece of sad news I tried to find an anchor to my tired and broken spirit. The world turned in my eyes into a black wave, as if the midday sun turned dark and the whole universe rolled and fell into a deep and dark abyss. The metaphor of the world standing on the brink[79] appeared real. The Talmud language has a special expression to this state: "*Gehinnom* is opening beneath him."[80]

---

77 He is referring to a well know Hebrew proverb: The tragedy of the many is half a measure of consolation.
78 A common Talmudic expression.
79 A Talmudic metaphor implying that the world is not standing on solid foundations but rather being held up by the strength of God's arms.
80 E.g., Rashi on Gen. 27:33:1.

Did I cry?—Not really. My heart froze, as if ceased sensing anything and my tongue was squeezed like in a vise. At that moment my eyes caught sight of the newspaper that was on the table. It turned black throughout. I could not distinguish between lines and letters. But suddenly my eyes recovered their light:[81] a black frame stood out of the black cloth; its color did not blend with the color of its surroundings. And inside that frame my eyes noticed lines, words and recognizable acronyms. And just then my eyes opened, I read and I understood. Hillel Zeitlin's[82] only daughter ת.נ.צ.ב.ה[83] died at the age of 29.

[An inverted note at the bottom of the page asks the recipient "if Zalman's sons do not collect stamps please return the stamps for my son."]

2

And I read and realized that my brother died at the age of 31; may his soul be bound up in the bond of everlasting life. That was the beginning of my consolation. After that I could write you the postcard. The sky started clearing up. The world and its surroundings started returning slowly to their normal shape. The sun shone again and life returned to its tracks. This was the half a measure of consolation that we need to accept from the divine.

---

81 A Talmudic expression.
82 A well-known Yiddish and Hebrew writer and poet 1871–1942.
83 ת.נ.צ.ב.ה: "May her soul be bound up in the bond of everlasting life."

Also: in truth, a man carries in him from birth the seed of death. We are dying every day, always, every hour. Death is incapsulated in our lives like the bitterness of an onion within its layers. Every day, hour by hour, we sense that our life is diminishing. Moment by moment, a layer is being shed and we are getting closer to the "bitter death."[84] You might not like my metaphor. It might not resemble the subject [death]. But you must admit that all the two billion and seven hundred million people who are walking the earth are approaching death every moment. In the end each one will taste the final and ultimate death. There is no escape. In my childhood I thought I would never die. I will be the exception . . . but by now that naïve belief has dissipated . . . . In our case the tragedy is that first of all, he [Shimon] is one of us. We had a brother and now no more. And the second, that a sharp knife peeled off the layers without mercy and surprisingly fast. He died prematurely. Our brother tasted the onion's bitter core before his time, rather than, by our expectations and desire, bit by bit over additional forty solar cycles. This tragedy—which is not unique just to us—is what enhances our grief, from which we will need to find shelter in the course of life.

[two lines are illegible]

Every individual, every creature is—as you know—an element of the general enterprise that is called the world. The earth, all that is on its inside and outside are one entity, one unit, that does not include death at all. From a biological point of view, from the scientific point of view, there is no death in the world at all. There are only chemical

---

84 1 Sam. 15:32.

changes. The world takes off one form and puts on another. Changes and variations occur every minute, every second, ceaselessly. The chemical and biological elements stay forever. You certainly remember Bialik's words in his poem "The Cemetery":

> For by aid of all we thrive. Life endless shall be thine,
> To blossom forth a flower or be woven in a vine.[85]

Although we all carry wishes, aspirations and unique characteristics, we are in fact nothing but one body with many shapes: the thinnest of all grains of sand or the 30 meter[86] long whale—all have the same value in the world of nature. And just like the water droplet that evaporated was never lost, nor did it die, it just turned into a gas, so is the man when he dies, his evolved shape as we perceive it, has merely changed. "The dead who lives" is not such a mysterious matter. And don't laugh at me and my "clumsiness." Please hold off your mockery. Just understand my dears the truth in these words! Remember Spinoza's[87] words:

> "Don't cry and don't laugh. Just observe and understand."[88]

---

[85] H. N. Bialik, *Poems from the Hebrew*, ed. L. V. Snowman (London: "Hasefer," 1924), 39, https://archive.org/details/ChaimNachman BialikPoemsFromTheHebrew/page/n1/mode/2up.

[86] Approximately thirty yards.

[87] Baruch Spinoza 1632–1677.

[88] The actual line is: "Don't cry and don't rage. Understand."

3

As was said, a person must rise above the minor daily details and look at eternity with open eyes. So did the Talmud sages when they modified the blessing "Blessed the True Judge,"[89] and Job said: "The Lord has given and the Lord has taken away."[90] And the clerics who changed the verses of acceptance of the lot like "The Rock!—His deeds are perfect."[91] They intended to give a person solace and redemption by looking at eternity through philosophical observations of the rules of life. Even religious terms such as the "world to come" and the "resurrection of the dead" are integrated into this view. It follows that we are not mourning the murky matter of our brother—that is not what we are mourning, that did not die. It will come back as a bud, or a tree, and will transform thousands of times and will change shapes and appearances endlessly. We are mourning the loss of our brother of blessed memory spiritual form.

We are mourning the death of the pure soul that once lived in that matter. For the departure of wisdom and will, feelings, the ability to move and speak—everything that we call a living person, or a person's life. But excessive mourning is strictly forbidden. "All who add, detract,"[92] this is grave sin against

---

[89] I.e., the rule that one must accept the bad things just as he accepts the good things and bless them accordingly.
[90] Job 1:21.
[91] Deut. 32:4.
[92] A Talmudic expression, e.g., Sefer HaMiddot, Truth, Part I 5.

nature, a criminal offense against human dignity. Because everybody is graced with the love of life, the instinct of survival. We must preserve that instinct and aspiration within us. Just see how the sages of the Talmud warned people against excessive mourning. We must believe that life has value. And while our brother was alive, his life had value to him and to us. We need to remember that in the perspective of our own lives and their value. We need to believe that there is a need for our lives, here on earth, as prescribed by our fate. We need to believe in the sanctity of his life.... But "The King is Dead—Long Live the King!"

The memory of our brother is particularly dear to us because he died childless and disappointed. We will try to preserve his memory as appropriate to self-respecting and wise people. His name, memory, and good deeds will live in our consciousness as a symbol of innocence, a pure and gentle soul, which was offered on the altar of love. He will continue living for us in this spiritual image. Because he was indeed a sacrifice on this altar. Love was the source of his life on this earth. His roots were nurtured by that source. And when that source died out, the nurturing of his pure soul died out too. Our brother could love with his entire soul. He died tormented by love. Not everyone merits that. This is an extremely high degree. Must be that his soul was carved from the heavens as the symbol of purity. We are proud of that. He was refined and purified by the heat of the pyre of love, in his life and at death. Let us keep the memory of his life not with gloom or grief, but with pride and reverence. Our salty tears will add nothing to us or to honor his memory. Get strong and cheer up. On the day I got your first notification I drafted a poem of "eulogy" to our brother, of blessed memory, which I am attaching. Writing this poem helped to fortify my depressed spirit. I hope it will help you cheer up and distract your aching heart from this great pain.

Eulogy

Alas, your heart was a fountain of lofty aspiration,
> Your soul aspired to supreme and noble beauty;
> But this spiritual aspiration and yearning
> Transformed a woman's beauty into source of sorrow.

Alas, feeling grief and anguish you kept your virtue
> And you trusted it to be certainly achievable
> But you did not understand that life's purpose
> Is not to achieve, but merely to aspire . . . .

Alas, for your soul was a vessel of purity and innocence
> In the chalice of your youthful heart, a great faith simmered
> A flawless sacrifice you offered in youthful silence
> The splendor of longing you took to your grave.

Well, my dears, we return to life. It is time we told each other about our own lives. How good and how pleasant it is that brothers dwell together[93] under the tree of love! How strongly

---

93 Ps. 133:1.

my soul yearned to read your written conversation because verbal conversation is impossible. How good would it be if it was under different circumstances, more joyful. Too bad that such a tragic occasion had to be the intermediary, that sweetness came forth of such a bitter occasion.[94] But what's done is done. What has happened has happened. I don't know how you comprehend this matter. I think that there is some consolation in this view. We lost a dear brother, but through this irreplaceable loss we found each other after so many years. It might be that if not for this loss, we would not have found each other ever. These are terrible matters. I admit that they have no logic or reason. The truth must be said without fear. If there is an afterlife, as millions of people believed and still believe—including learned and wise people—that the soul continues to live a conscious and knowledgeable life even after leaving the body, then the soul of our brother knows about our getting closer that his death caused—it must experience joy knowing that it happened at his own hands.... It must know that on the day of its departure and separation from his body our three hearts came together in an oath to remain faithful to each other. That's life my dears. Good follows the bad. Joy follows grief....

Let's not dwell my dears on the former things. Let's not look at the pointless details of the reasons that separated us. Some of them are clearly known: the distance, the Brazilian lifestyle, the hardships of my own life. These are the knowns. And as for the concealed—better leave them concealed. Let's forgive each other's insults. Forget them. If it was decreed that

---

94   A reference to "Out of the strong came forth sweetness," Judg. 14:14.

the dead be forgotten—these certainly can be forgotten. Great satisfaction accompanied by great sorrow rushed through my heart as I read your confessions. Satisfaction for learning that finally you recognized that spirituality could bring you happiness in life.

[This is the end of this page. The remaining page(s) are missing.]

Letter to His Mother[95]

Międzyrzecz, Tuesday, 28 Adar II, 5695[96]
Dear Mother!

Thank you for your letter. We were glad to hear about your health. I know that you never forget us, that your love for us is great, that you would like to see the best for us, and that you are always ready to express your feelings with tangible support. I'm sorry you're worrying about us, that you're suffering because you know our situation. Believe me, I have never aspired to become rich. I'm content with little. I probably inherited that inclination from my father, may he rest in peace, and maybe I was also influenced by the holy books I studied so intensively in the best years of my life. However, I would be happy to be rich if it meant that you wouldn't have to worry about me... but it's of no use, I can't do anything about it. The world is not a store where one can buy whatever one's heart desires. Instead, it's all about haggling and bargaining. I'm writing this to encourage you not to fret about our situation. Probably it's meant to be so.

[One line is missing]

[...] and words cannot express to you my heartfelt thanks. But one does not thank a mother. A mother does not give out of generosity. She does so because she is a mother. I believe, however, that there are many mothers who worry less about

---

95 From the collection of Avrom Bendavid-Val; translated from Yiddish by Ellen Cassedy.
96 April 2, 1935.

their grown children. If you meet with your brother, give him our greetings. I would have written him, but unfortunately, I don't speak English.

Ya'akov is a dear brother. I have no complaints about him. He writes to me often and is pleased with my answers. He often asks for advice about his situation, he confides in me about his troubles and his joys—to me that is worth its weight in gold. And sometimes he sends me money. True, he doesn't send much, but I know he does it with all his heart. I don't actually need anything from him. He sends the money out of his own need to show his feeling for me. This winter he sent me 5 dollars and Shifra 3 dollars.

I can't say the same about my Brazilian brothers. We are like strangers, as if we don't exist for one another, as if we had not grown up together, not been born to the same mother, not suckled at the same breast, not educated in the same faith, not studied the same books, not traveled together, not experienced the same joys and tribulations, not had the same hopes for the future, and not aspired to the same goals or cherished the same ideals. But if they have forgotten—how can I forget? They're involved in a foreign world of bargaining and commerce, have replaced their books for a merchant's license, have pursued a material fortune and abandoned the spiritual wealth of Torah and justice they absorbed in our house. And in so doing, they, my brothers and sisters, have ripped out of their hearts and erased from their minds all traces of their flesh and blood.

Of them all, I'm most annoyed with Zalman. I've learned that he is making a living—a better living than mine. I don't care about his wealth. I don't expect any help from him. But where is his brotherly feeling? Is his heart so full of profits that there's no room for his own brother? And after all that I did for him? In Kishinev, and later at home, and in Lutsk and in Rovno—we breathed the same air, we both chopped wood in the winter to earn a crust of bread. Should I forget how I went on foot to Kolky, to Olyka and Lutsk, to have the officer get him out of the military? Should I forget the endless reams of papers I've written officially on his account, to secure his education, in order to teach him? This is why I have so much pain when I think of him. Yes, Shimon and Naftali also owe me more than a little debt.

But it is my misfortune to be their father after our father's death. I comforted them and supported them, renouncing my last hard-earned morsel of bread for them, all out the goodness of my heart. How have they forgotten all this?

I often receive letters from Shifra. We write to each other every two weeks. I don't hear as often from Hershele,[97] but we're not on bad terms. He lives in a small town near Rovno and makes a good living as both a ritual slaughterer and a rabbi. I also hear often from YomTov. I haven't heard from Surkeh[98] and Shifrele for several months. At the beginning of the winter, I had a letter from her, in which she complained that her children were sick. I wrote back right away, but I haven't heard from her since then. I wrote several letters to Yisroel Fuchs[?], and he and his wife wrote back warmly several times, but they complained that times are hard for them.

---

97 One of the brothers, Zvi Hirsch.
98 The oldest sister Sarah who immigrated to New York.

Don't be angry that I've written so much about the Brazilians. Sometimes I need to get this off my chest. Maybe you will decide whether to write to them or to send them my letter. Maybe my words would have an effect on them, because "words that come from the heart enter the heart," and their feelings of love will be awakened. I beg you to convey a heartfelt greeting to Rebbe Rubinstein and his whole household. Beyltshe sends you kisses $g"p$.[99] My children are healthy as usual, thank God, and they are good students.

I wish you a kosher and a happy holiday [Passover].

Your Yisrael

---

99 In Hebrew פ"ג—three times, i.e., three kisses.

References

Aleichem, Sholom. *Some Laughter, Some Tears: Tales from the Old World and the New.* Selected and translated, with an introduction by Curt Leviatan. New York: G.P. Putnam's Sons, 1968.

Bendavid-Val, Avrom. *The Heavens Are Empty: Discovering the Lost Town of Trochenbrod.* New York: Pegasus Books, 2011.

Gold, Betty, and Mark Hodermarsky. *Beyond Trochenbrod: The Betty Gold Story.* Kent, OH: The Kent State University Press, 2014.

Laufer, Gabriel. *A Survivor's Duty—Surviving the Holocaust and Fighting for Israel: A story of Father and Son.* Boston: Indiana University Press, 2018.

Pick, Aharon. *Notes from the Valley of Slaughter: A Memoir, Written in the Ghetto of Šiauliai (Lithuania), 1942–44.* Translated by Gabriel Laufer. Bloomington, IN: Indiana University Press, 2023.

Safran Foer, Jonathan. *Everything Is Illuminated.* Boston: Houghton Mifflin, 2002.

Vainer, Ya'akov et al., eds. *Ha-Ilan ve-Shorashav: Sefer Korot Tal: Zofyovka—Ignatovka* [The tree and its roots: history book of Tal: Sofiovka—Ignatovka]. Giv'atayim: Agudat Bet Tal, 1988.

Appendix: Yisrael Beider's Family Tree,

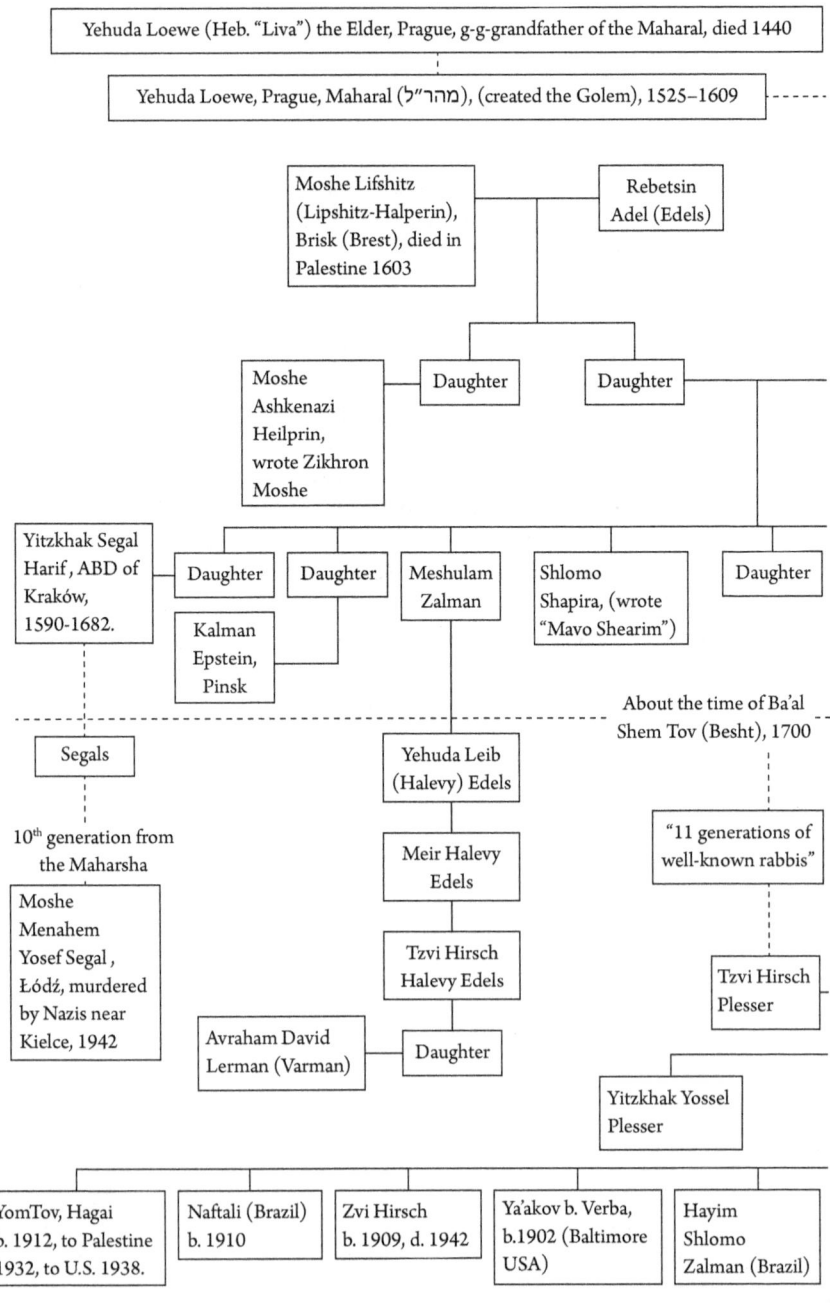

Prepared by Avrom Bendavid-Val, June 28, 2012

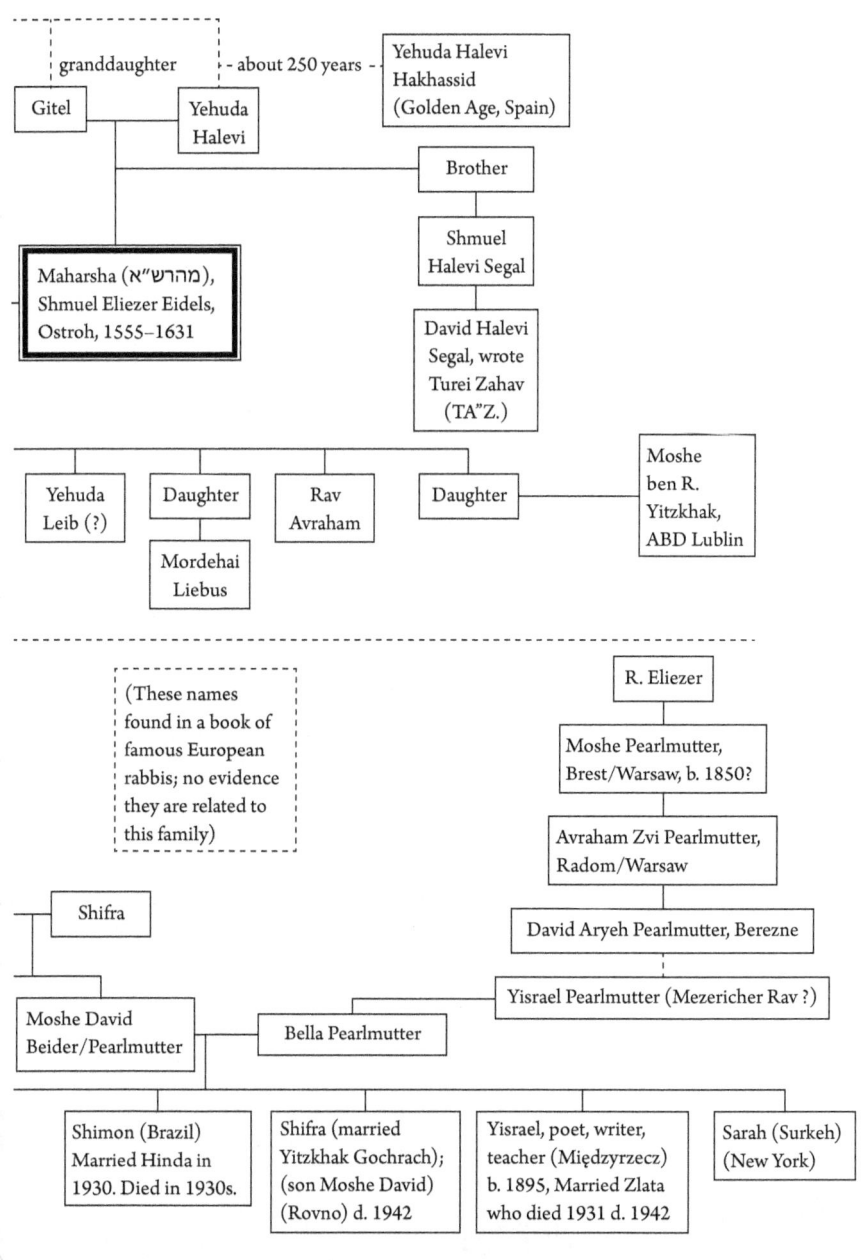

www.ingramcontent.com/pod-product-compliance
Lightning Source LLC
Chambersburg PA
CBHW050859160426
43194CB00011B/2221